Lady Gaga
Just Dance:
The Biography

Lady Gaga
Just Dance:
The Biography

Helia Phoenix

For all the little monsters who understand that you
can never love music enough

the auth   ice with the

This edition first published in Great Britain in 2010 by
Orion Books
an imprint of the Orion Publishing Group Ltd
Orion House, 5 Upper St Martin's Lane,
London WC2H 9EA
An Hachette Livre UK Company

1 3 5 7 9 10 8 6 4 2

A CIP catalogue record for this book is available
from the British Library.

ISBN: 9781409115670 (hardback)
9781409115687 (export trade paperback)

Printed in Great Britain by Clays Ltd. St Ives plc

The Orion Publishing Group's policy is to use papers that are natural, renewable
and recyclable and made from wood grown in sustainable forests. The logging and
manufacturing processes are expected to conform to the environmental
regulations of the country of origin.

Every effort has been made to fulfil requirements with regard to reproducing
copyright material. The author and publisher will be glad to rectify any omissions
at the earliest opportunity.

www.orionbooks.co.uk

Contents

List of illustrations

Section 1

Lady Gaga performing at the New Year's Eve Ball at Webster Hall on 31 December 2008 in New York City. (Photo by Neilson Barnard/Getty Images)

Posing with dancers Louis Loggerfeld, Tony Ferris, Duke Jones, and Micky Mugler after their performance at Interscope Geffen A&M Records Host American Music Awards After Party at Boulevard3 on 23 November 2008 in Hollywood, California. (Photo by Brian To/FilmMagic)

Backstage at the Y 100 Jingle Ball held at Bank Atlantic Center on 13 December 2008 in Sunrise, Florida. (Photo by Larry Marano/Getty Images)

Arriving at The Dome 47 music show at the SAP Arena on 29 August 2008 in Mannheim, Germany. (Photo by Anne-Laure Fontaine/WireImage)

Lady Gaga

Attending the 13th Annual ACE Awards presented by the Accessories Council at Cipriani 42nd Street on 2 November 2009 in New York City. (Photo by Dimitrios Kambouris/Getty Images for The Accessories Council)

Arriving at 102.7 KIIS-FM's Wango Tango 2009 at the Verizon Wireless Amphitheater on 9 May 2009 in Irvine, California. (Photo by Jesse Grant/WireImage)

Posing backstage during the Brit Awards 2009 at Earls Court on 18 February 2009 in London. (Photo by Tim Whitby/Getty Images)

With Paris Hilton at the Nokia 5800 launch party, Punk nightclub, London on 27 January 2009, where she performed her single 'Just Dance'. (Photo by Dave M. Benett/Getty Images)

Section 2

Lady Gaga performing onstage at 102.7 KIIS-FM's Wango Tango at Verizon Wireless Amphitheater on 9 May 2009 in Irvine, California. (Photo by Jason LaVeris/FilmMagic)

Performing during Perez Hilton's 'One Night in' concert series at Highline Ballroom on 24 October 2008 in New York City. (Photo by Bennett Raglin/WireImage)

Onstage at the 2009 American Music Awards at Nokia Theatre L.A. Live on 22 November 2009 in Los Angeles, California. (Photo by Kevin Winter/AMA2009/Getty Images for DCP)

Appearing live on American Idol on 1 April 2009 in Los Angeles, California. (Photo by F Micelotta/American Idol 2009/Getty Images for Fox)

Performing at The GRAMMY Celebration Concert Tour presented by T-Mobile Sidekick at House of Blues in Boston, MA on 4 May 2009. (Photo by Chris Polk/FilmMagic)

Arriving at the MTV Video Music Awards at Radio City Music Hall on 13 September 2009 in New York City. (Photo by Michael Loccisano/Getty Images)

With Kermit the frog at the MTV Awards. (Photo by Kevin Mazur/WireImage)

Posing in the pressroom during the MTV Awards. (Photo by Michael Loccisano/Getty Images)

Performing onstage during the MTV Awards. (Photo by Kevin Mazur/WireImage)

Section 3

Lady Gaga performing at the launch of V61 hosted by V Magazine, Marc Jacobs and Belvedere Vodka on 14 September 2009 in New York City. (Photo by Stephen Lovekin/Getty Images)

In concert at DAR Constitution Hall on 29 September 2009 in Washington, DC. (Photo by Paul Morigi/WireImage)

At the Open A.I.R. Summer Concert Series presented by Atlas New York on 15 May 2008 (Photo by Theo Wargo/WireImage)

Performing during the MOCA NEW 30th anniversary gala held at MOCA on 14 November 2009 in Los Angeles, California. (Photo by Michael Caulfield/Getty Images for MOCA)

Presenting cooperation with 'Monster Cable' at IFA fair on 7 September 2009 in Berlin, Germany. (Photo by Florian Seefried/ Getty Images)

Attending the Monster Cable party at Tube Station on 7 September 2009 in Berlin, Germany. (Photo by Florian Seefried/Getty Images)

Posing backstage during MTV's Total Request Live at the MTV Times Square Studios on 12 August 2008 in New York City. (Photo by Scott Gries/Getty Images)

Performing during the MOCA NEW 30th anniversary gala held at MOCA on 14 November 2009 in Los Angeles, California. (Photo by Michael Caulfield/Getty Images for MOCA)

Appearing at the 20th Annual MuchMusic Video Awards at the MuchMusic HQ on 21 June, 2009 in Toronto, Canada. (Photo by George Pimentel/WireImage)

Accepting her award onstage during the 2009 MTV Video Music Awards at Radio City Music Hall on 13 September, 2009 in New York City. (Photo by Jeff Kravitz/FilmMagic)

Acknowledgements

This book is dedicated to a lot of people, but in particular my mum, who never let me forget that writing was my dream. And for looking after me whenever I needed a break from myself.

This book would never have been possible without the constant love, support and cups of tea from Shane, who also helped me realise when it was time to take a mental bath and leave the work alone for a while.

Special thanks to Hannah, for being a constant source of inspiration throughout the writing of this book, and being a good friend from Cardiff to Berkeley and beyond. More thanks to Pamela, for seeing me through this project with kind words, and for friendship through the years.

Milly and Jane and all at Orion - thanks for all your help with this book and being such a great team. Helen Pope and

Lady Gaga

Ishmael Reed – thanks for being the best teachers I ever had. General thanks to all family and friends for being amazing – Cardiff crew, Kruger folk, 'sisters' – all of you. This book is also dedicated to the memory of my special friend Geoff.

A final special thank you to Lady Gaga: for bringing the intelligence, cool and amazingness back to pop. Keep up the good work – the charts wouldn't be the same without you.

Chapter One
A Star is Born

Stefani squealed with joy as her father picked her up and twirled her around to the music while a Bruce Springsteen record spun on the record player in the living room. Beside it rested records by Pink Floyd, Led Zeppelin, The Beatles, Billy Joel, the Rolling Stones and Elton John – all of which her daddy loved to play while dancing around with his daughter.

Born on 28 March 1986 in Yonkers, New York, Stefani Joanne Angelina Germanotta was always surrounded by music. She even grew up two blocks from John Lennon's memorial in New York City, and close to the Dakota, an apartment block by Central Park where John lived with Yoko Ono when he was shot.

Even mealtimes were a musical affair in the Germanotta household. Because of her family's Italian heritage there was always tasty Italian food in the house, such as meatballs and marinara, but while eating, the family would listen to records by the Italian opera singer Andrea Bocelli or Frank Sinatra, whose parents were Italian immigrants.

It was at this tender age, while listening to Frank Sinatra's duets on repeat with her father, that the young star-to-be became interested in theatre. She was always a daddy's girl, and loved nothing more than hanging out by the record player with him, listening to Sinatra singing along with Gladys Knight and Stevie Wonder in 'For Once in My Life' or Sinatra and Luis Miguel dueting on 'Come Fly With Me'.

Her Italian American parents were loving and supportive, and wanted their daughters Stefani and her little sister Natali to pursue their dreams. Dad Joseph was an Internet entrepreneur and mum Cynthia worked in telecommunications. The family was pretty well off and lived in New York's Upper West Side, so Stefani and her sister had pretty much everything they wanted as children. Despite Stefani remembering having a really amazing childhood, her parents didn't spoil their daughters. They were hard working and wanted to raise them to be driven, respectful and appreciative of what they had.

One way Cynthia decided to do this with Stefani was to make her learn to play piano. She wanted her daughter to learn an instrument because she loved music, but also to instill a sense of discipline in her. Young Stefani didn't want to practise, but mum was determined that she would sit at the piano, whether she practised or not.

'You don't have to practise, but you have to sit there for an hour a day. You don't have to play – but you have to sit there,' she told her daughter. Stefani banged her fists on the keys in protest, remembering later: 'I was a really bad kid!'

Her mother wouldn't budge, though. After days of sitting

at the piano with her arms folded, eventually Stefani got bored and started to play. She loved playing the piano, she just hated lessons and practising her scales. Stefani loved to play by ear, which she found much easier, but the practice paid off in the end. She learned fast and became very good at classical piano very quickly.

One thing is for sure, when mum Cynthia made her four-year-old daughter sit at the piano until she learned how to play it, she had no idea that nearly twenty years later her daughter would be playing it in front of thousands of fans – pretty much in her birthday suit. She also had no idea that by this time everyone, including her, would call her daughter by a different name: Lady Gaga.

Young Stefani got a taste for shocking people from a very young age, which included an incident where she greeted the babysitter at the door – so innocently – completely naked. 'I discovered my love of shock art at an early age,' she has said. 'I always wanted to be a star. I always wanted to be some kind of commercial vehicle that had the attention of the world and could say and do things to inspire people. That's just always been what I wanted to do.'

She certainly made sure she got plenty of practice, singing along to Michael Jackson, Madonna and Cyndi Lauper on her plastic toy tape recorder. She was deeply influenced by pop music and loved watching shows like the MTV Video Music Awards on television. She would wrap a big blanket around herself – an Afghan that her grandmother had knitted – and wear it like a gown. 'I would run around the basement with popcorn and scream in excitement waiting for them to come on,' she remembered later when speaking to *Newsweek*. 'I used to love the big pop acts. I remember Alicia Keys gave a beautiful performance and Michael Jackson with *NSYNC.'

Her love of performing started early too. When her parents used to go out to eat at fancy Upper West Side restaurants, she would dance around the table using the breadsticks as a baton.

She was always an entertainer, describing herself as 'a ham' when she was a little girl. 'Some people are just born stars,' she later told the *News of the World*'s magazine *Fabulous*. 'You either have it or you haven't, and I was definitely born one. Even as a kid I always had eyes on me, like bees on honey. I was always outrageous and I was always very smart.'

It was at the same tender age that this outrageous, smart kid started experimenting with do-it-yourself costume design and fashion. Her very first performance in first grade was in *The Billy Goats Gruff*, where she had won the part of the big billy goat.

Stefani decided that no shop-bought costume would do, and nor would she use papier mâché, like all the other kids in her class. Instead, she made her billy-goat horns herself out of tin-foil and clothes hangers. Needless to say, she was the star of the show.

Stefani was already absorbing her mother's fine taste in clothes, a passion they would come to share in the future. Mom Cynthia had a real love of fashion and classic Italian taste, and she regularly wore designers like Salvatore Ferragamo, Valentino and Paloma Picasso.

Stefani's baby sister Natali noticed her older sibling's determination and ambition when they were kids. 'We would fight, and she would say, "Why do you always have to be the best?"' Gaga recalled in 2008 on one of her *Transmission* videos. 'She doesn't any more. Now she's like, "Be the best! I love it when you're the best!" I don't know who wants to be second.'

4

Being second was definitely not an option for Stefani. Whatever she did, she gave it her all, and wasn't happy until she'd achieved the best she possibly could. This translated into a tough work ethic for homework and an even tougher one when it came to music.

Although many youngsters grow out of their desire to be stars once they go to high school, Gaga did not. Having enrolled in an exclusive private school in Manhattan, she was about to rub shoulders with some pretty famous students.

Chapter Two
Catholic Schoolgirls

Stefani's parents sent her to Convent of the Sacred Heart, the oldest independent girls' school in Manhattan. The school was founded in 1881 by the Society of the Sacred Heart, nuns who were dedicated to educating the daughters of upper-class Catholic families.

Attending Convent of the Sacred Heart was a pretty big deal. Set in two elaborate mansions on the Upper East Side, the private girls-only school was one of the most selective in New York, and cost around £23,000 a year to attend. Having made money from their Internet business, Stefani's parents wanted their daughter to have the best education money could buy.

The school had some pretty famous students even before Stefani arrived, such as Caroline Kennedy (daughter of assassinated president John Kennedy) and actress Jordana Brewster (who appeared in *The Fast and the Furious*). And that's not to mention Sacred Heart's most famous pupils, until Gaga came along of course: Paris and Nicky Hilton.

The school has also been name-checked in quite a few films; the girls in the film *Nick & Norah's Infinite Playlist* attended Sacred Heart, for example. The girls at the school were living the life that many dream of. The annual prom looked like a Ralph Lauren runway, with some of the most privileged young ladies in the world in attendance.

Back when Sacred Heart was started, the school taught classes designed to educate young ladies in social graces and appropriate behaviour, requiring a curriculum of politeness, French and art, amongst other things.

Over a hundred years later, the school has modernised quite a bit. Sister Nancy Salisbury, who was the headmistress when Stefani started, was determined that all the girls attending would have a thorough education, which meant teaching them about important issues as well as their ABCs. Students therefore attended classes in economics, politics, sex education and computing, as well as an improved arts programme.

This made it perfect for young Stefani, who was determined to pursue her love of music. So, alongside the usual boring literary and mathematics classes, she got to focus on studying piano, voice and drama – three things she was already mad about. She would wander between classes, walking on thick carpets and polished wooden floors, surrounded by ornate marble statues and sweeping staircases. It was more like the set from a lavish musical or film set than the sort of place you expect to find hundreds of schoolgirls wandering around. But it was in just this setting that Stefani began her education as a teenager, and began on her voyage of self-discovery into adulthood.

*

Considering the sorts of girls who attended, it's no wonder that Sacred Heart is the inspiration for so many teen TV series and books. Set in two huge mansions on New York's exclusive Fifth Avenue, and with marble staircases and cherubs decorating the outside walls, rumour has it that the TV series *Gossip Girl* was based on Sacred Heart. The action in *Gossip Girl* – drugs, drinking and unfaithful boyfriends and girlfriends – is rumoured to be all the rage at Manhattan's top private schools.

Even though the rumour mill has plenty of stories about the Sacred Heart girls' wild behaviour, in reality the school was very strict, with traditional rules to keep the girls in line. When Stefani was dropped off at the school in the morning, for example, a Sister would greet her and Stefani would have to curtsy to her.

As a Catholic school, much of what Sacred Heart taught was based on religion, morality and discipline – quite the opposite of what Lady Gaga's public persona would turn out to be. The uniform was strict too. In the upper school, the girls had to wear blue cotton skirts in the summer and kilts in the winter. The Sisters even had a measuring stick, to ensure that skirts were the right length. In the lower school, the younger girls had to wear red and white checked pinafores with a grey tunic and blue shorts to preserve their modesty. It's almost certain that this strict environment had an influence on the future style of Lady Gaga and her outlandish choice of dress.

Although Stefani claims she didn't follow the dress code and used to dress differently from the other girls, her friends insist that she was quite well behaved at school.

'We were a rich kids' school but with good morals,' remembered Cristina Civetta, a New York writer and fashion designer who went to Sacred Heart with Stefani, and attended a religious retreat at a New York monastery with her while they were there. 'Stefani was a straight-A student who wore her skirt to her knee, as we were supposed to, and knee-high socks. Stefani is a good girl, really sweet and normal,' she added when talking to the *Daily Mail*.

Even though the list of students at Sacred Heart read like a *Who's Who* of high society, Stefani wasn't in with the in-crowd there. Paris and Nicky Hilton attended the school but were a couple of years older than Stefani. In fact, by the time she started at Sacred Heart Paris had already left to attend another exclusive New York private school, Dwight School, for her junior and sophomore years. Stefani would only ever see Nicky between classes by the lockers in the hallway, and didn't really know her.

But though she never hung out with Nicky or her high society friends, Stefani learned about them from a distance – enough to teach her about being herself. Her memories of them are that they were 'pretty, and very clean. Very, very clean.' But she was impressed with how perfect they were all the time – with their hair and make-up flawlessly done. She would catch glimpses of them preening themselves in the marble-floored bathrooms at school, and found them fascinating creatures to observe.

'What I think was interesting about going to that school was that there were some girls that had tons of money, some that had no money, some down the middle,' Stefani told gay magazine *Fab*. 'There were blondes, brunettes, artsy girls, stoner girls, we had everybody.'

There was certainly a mix of people at the school, but while there were a few rebels, Stefani wasn't one of them. According to one of her old friends, one girl got drunk and punched Sister Nancy so hard she knocked the nun out, but bad behaviour like that was rare. Stefani and her schoolmates had to complete four hours of homework every night, so there was little time for going out and going crazy during the week.

So if Stefani wasn't the prettiest or the most popular girl at the school, where did she fit in amongst the elite? The truth is, she didn't. In 2007 she told *Women's Wear Daily* that the girls at school used to tease her, saying, 'What are you, a lesbian? No one's looking at you.'

She described herself as a 'weird girl' in school, who did theatre, sang in choirs and bands, would come to school with lashings of red lipstick on, or with her hair arranged strangely, 'or whatever I was doing to get attention' she later laughed in an interview with About.com.

She was more interested in art and music than she was in boys – something a lot of girls found pretty weird. But it was her studies of history and music that she really loved, so she devoted herself to them. She continued to practise the piano, at which she'd become very good, and learned the harmonica a little, too.

However, there was a key moment in her young life that was to put her firmly on the path to future superstardom – a moment where fate stepped in to lend her a hand.

Chapter Three
Fate Lends an Ear

After school one day, Stefani was in a boutique in downtown New York. As she browsed the neon tutus and brightly coloured slash-neck shirts in the store, she absent-mindedly sang to herself, not realising that anyone was listening. But somebody was. One of the store's employees, called Evan, heard her singing, and asked her if she was a singer. She giggled and said no, shyly, but Evan was impressed with her voice. He told Stefani that she should contact his uncle, as his uncle was a voice teacher.

Stefani couldn't believe it. It seemed like such a great opportunity. But she checked her enthusiasm. The voice coach was probably just some amateur who taught singing for fun. But she got the number, went home and called Evan's uncle, who turned out to be non other than the legendary Don Lawrence, famous in the music business for being one of the most successful vocal coaches in the world. It was a very strange turn of fate that led Stefani to him – and once again, she felt like it was her destiny to be a star, and that Don would help her on her way.

Although he was very busy teaching and coaching the likes of Mick Jagger, Bono, Christina Aguilera, En Vogue, Annie Lennox, Beyoncé and many more, he managed to find time in his busy schedule for the talented little brunette with frizzy hair. Perhaps he saw in her a glimpse of what could happen in her future and the bright lights of stardom that would beckon in a few years' time.

Convinced that Stefani was capable of achieving great things, Don made sure he found time to advise her on how to develop as an artist as well as just a singer. Don became more than just a teacher. He was like a guru, and would remain a constant presence right through to her big break into showbiz, and beyond. Knowing that she possessed a very special musical talent, he encouraged the youngster to develop and push her own limits.

'He was my mentor. He still is my mentor,' she later said. 'He encouraged me to start writing music. Around thirteen I started writing music, stuff on the piano in my house, so I moved from classical to pop, and I started noticing that the Bach chords are the same chords as in this Mariah Carey record … so I just started picking up on little things, doing small chord progressions.'

All the practise paid off. Spending increasingly more and more time tinkling the ivories on the piano in the backroom at home, Stefani wrote her first piano ballad soon after meeting Don, and continued to work on her songs. Back then though, her songs were influenced by artists like Carole King and Patti Smith, and this showed in her sweet song-writing style.

Don was a source of support and inspiration throughout Stefani's journey from awkward teenager to fully formed pop princess. In the liner notes to her album *The Fame*, she gives a special mention to him: 'You are the greatest and most gifted teacher I ever had. Thank you for my voice, my work ethic, and my discipline.' It's hard to imagine whether she might have made it without Don to help her on the way.

With Don's encouragement, she started looking for other places to practise her skills. Walking down the marble corridors at school one day, she noticed a sign pinned to a noticeboard, advertising a school singing group called the Madrigals. The group would sometimes rehearse at 7.30am, and so only attracted girls who were serious about their singing.

So Stefani's love of music and performing didn't die at high school. Her appetite for listening to music just grew and grew. She loved Grace Jones for her innovative fashion style and great songs – she particularly loved her songs 'Slave to the Rhythm' and 'Corporate Cannibal'. She would listen to Madonna's *Immaculate Collection* CD on repeat, and dance around her bedroom, twirling and copying the dance moves from 'Vogue'. David Bowie and Queen were also on her stereo, almost obsessively. All four artists would go on to be hugely influential on the future Lady Gaga's music and her style.

Stefani was proud to wear her love of music on her sleeve – literally. She had a leather jacket with a Hanson pin on it, and a t-shirt that said "I love Donnie!", proclaiming her love for Donnie from New Kids On The Block. She could never have imagined that in a few years time she would be friends with

New Kids – going on tour with them and writing songs for them.

She loved all kinds of music – from the 1970s rock that her father had played her as a child, to the ska-influenced punk pop of Greenday and No Doubt that she would hear on the radio, to glistening power-pop in the charts.

Another artist she would later go on to write songs for was Britney Spears. Young Stefani and her friends were obsessed by Britney when she first became a star with raunchy tracks like 'Oops! … I Did It Again', listening to her songs over and over again.

Her love for Britney led her to try and catch glimpses of the singer when she would come to New York to perform or give interviews. After school one day when she knew Britney was going to be performing, Stefani and her friends jumped onto a crammed subway carriage and took the train down-town, running from the station to the glitzy MTV studios where *TRL* [Total Request Live – an MTV series] was being filmed. Stefani – who loved the singer – had Britney's name written in glitter on her face, as did some of her friends. The girls pushed to the front of the crowd and screamed with excitement, hoping they would see a famous hand or a face in the windows of the studio.

She later told *Maxim* magazine that she was 'amazed by the level of superfan that Britney created. I liked to watch the hyperventilating'. As Lady Gaga, she says now that she looks back on those days fondly. 'It doesn't happen any more, and it's quite sad. It's my intention to revive that lunacy with *The Fame*. You can't deny the power of a pop group being able to stop traffic.'

It was around this time this that Stefani started to get into fash-ion, wearing acid wash jeans and tank tops with sneakers. She was influenced by the styles of the 1950s, but also by the club scene, even though she was too young legally to set foot inside a club! Even at this young age she had the potential to shock, and it was now that she developed a taste for fishnets and bright red lipstick, a look she kept through the transformation from Stefani into Lady Gaga.

Even in her mid-teens, Stefani liked showing a bit of flesh – possibly as a reaction to the modest clothing all Sacred Heart students were forced to wear at school. 'When I was fifteen, I would wear stonewashed jeans with tight, midriff-showing tank tops,' she recalled, when being interviewed for *Maxim*. 'I had huge boobs, because I was 20 pounds heavier then. Big frizzy brown hair. Hot pink lipstick.' Although she was described by some as an ugly duckling, there was something about the teenager that made people stop and stare at her. She had a cer-tain something they couldn't put their finger on – a certain quality that attracted people's attention.

Stefani found the discipline and strict nature of Sacred Heart difficult to cope with. She was a good student and stud-ied hard, but felt that the school was stifling her creativity. 'I felt I couldn't be the real me,' she said about it later. 'But I re-alised you don't have to be a victim of your environment. Just because they told me how to be didn't mean I had to be that way for life. There was something else for me.'

That something else lay in her love of music and perform-ing. Attending a Catholic school, Stefani, who remained reli-gious after her transformation into Lady Gaga, noticed and loved the element of drama in religion.

Her performing was also getting her noticed at school.

Dressed in a ball gown, she walked solemnly down the sweeping marble staircase and into the elegantly decorated ballroom of Sacred Heart. She sat in front of the huge, antique grand piano at the front of the hall, and began to play classical piano for all the parents, nuns and fellow students who were attending a dinner there.

Stefani was also was a keen drama student, and appeared in many of the productions put on by Regis High School, a nearby Catholic boys' school that needed girls for its plays. Stefani played Alice More in *A Man for All Seasons,* Philia in *A Funny Thing Happened on the Way to the Forum*, and Anna Andreyevna in *The Government Inspector*. She also sang in productions of the Regis Jazz Band and in the Sacred Heart school choir, where she won the role of lead soprano.

According to Charlene Gianetti, whose daughter attended Sacred Heart at the same time as Stefani, everyone knew Stefani was destined to be a star: 'Her talent was so astounding, it literally took your breath away,' Charlene wrote on her blog. 'When she was a senior, she appeared as Adelaide in a production of *Guys and Dolls* staged at Regis High School, on East 84th Street. Since Regis is an all-boys school, it must import girls for its plays. They were fortunate to have enlisted Stefani. Now, the Regis boys are very smart (a rigorous exam and selection process is necessary for admission) and talented. But whenever Stefani was on stage, she stole the show.'

As she was only in her mid-teens, she was too young to play at bars or clubs. But she was desperate to perform her music live, so Stefani begged her mum to take her to open-mic nights in New York, where anyone could get up onstage and sing or play music for the audience. Her mum agreed, keen for her talented daughter to develop her skills. 'My parents always knew

I was going to be a performer, and they just wanted to help me pursue my passion. They never hindered my creativity,' Stefani told *New Times*.

Stefani and her mum found some jazz clubs and coffee houses in the Village that ran open-mic nights, but at first Cynthia had a difficult job persuading the staff to let them in because of Stefani's age. The doorman frowned, but Cynthia was determined. 'My daughter's very young but she's very talented,' she explained to him. 'I'll sit with her as she plays.'

Her persistence paid off. Stefani played beautifully, and because she was so talented she was always welcomed back. 'When I was fifteen and sixteen, I was getting a lot of attention for my voice and for my songwriting because I was so young,' Stefani recalled.

With new friends she had met at Regis High School, Stefani would start sneaking out to go downtown, just to experience the music nightlife in New York. And she was playing more and more coffee house open-mic nights. The kinds of places she loved frequenting were hardly appropriate places for a teenager attending such a prestigious school. The open-mic nights were usually in dark, busy dive bars, which stank of urine and had obscene graffiti scrawled over the often-flooded bathrooms. But they gave Stefani a taste of another life, which she was desperate to experience more of.

She also joined a cover band in her freshman year of high school, who would play many classic rock tracks – including songs by Led Zeppelin, Jefferson Airplane, and U2 amongst others. And it was around this time that rock'n'roll started to appeal to the bad side of the young, respectable, straight-A student. 'I met some good-looking guys with guitars, and I wanted to have sex with really hot older men – they were seniors!' she explained to *Rolling Stone*.

But her late nights weren't all about hot guys, though they were definitely a bonus. She was so busy with musicals and cover bands and choirs and open-mic nights that she was rarely home early. And although he wanted her to pursue her musical dream, her father was getting a little disturbed by the late nights. Unable to go to bed until he knew she was home safely, he would sit on the brown leather couch in the living room, pretending to watch TV until he heard the door open. 'My dad would be waiting for me to get home from a club, sweating … having a heart attack,' she said later, remembering the time. 'I didn't like upsetting him. But I did like being myself.'

When she wasn't upsetting her father by getting home late, she was studying hard at her classes at school, improving her knowledge of theatre and music, though she remained far away from Sacred Heart's social elite. As an Italian-American woman who was only the second in her generation to go to college, Stefani was proud of her education, and worked hard at it.

'I don't know that my schooling was conducive to wild ideas and creativity, but it gave me discipline, drive,' she later told the *Guardian*. 'They taught me how to think. I really know how to think. [For example] if I decide to make a coat red in the show, it's not just red. I think: is it communist red? Is it cherry cordial? Is it ruby red? Or is it apple red? Or the big red balloon red?

'I mean there's like so many f***ing different kinds of red. And so you have to say, well, what are we trying to say in this scene? Is it a happy red? Or a sad red? Is it a lace red? Or a leather red? Or a wool red? It's like there are so many components to making a show and making art, and my school taught me how to think that way,' she explained.

She remembers being teased about her unorthodox, occasionally attention-seeking style. 'For a little while I thought girls were just jealous, which is why they were mean to me,' she said later to *Entertainment Weekly*. 'Maybe they were jealous of my fearlessness. But I think I genuinely used to rub people up the wrong way. I'd talk about things and do things that were very ostentatious, and over the top, and very vain … When you're twelve years old and making clothes with plastic flowers attached to them, and trying to choreograph shows at your school that are entirely too sexy, you start to be like, OK, this is my aesthetic. My aesthetic is in so many ways exactly the same as it was when I was younger, I'm just smarter.'

Despite whatever teasing she suffered from the in-crowd, attending Sacred Heart gave her a lot and she remains pleased that she went there. 'Some girls were mean,' she said. 'They made fun of me because I dressed differently and played in bands. They couldn't work out why I was so driven. But there were times when I got a lot of attention for being the life and soul of the party.'

She might not have fit in with the likes of the Hiltons, but this artsy girl who got good grades learned the trick of reinvention at Sacred Heart – something that would come in handy during the transformation she was about to go through. Her style and look were out there, veering between overtly sexy and a bit strange. Stefani's girlfriends used to tell her that no matter what she was wearing, even zipped up to her neck in a parka, she looked naked. Perhaps it was because of this that she practically decided to abandon her clothes altogether while performing.

'I was the nerdy theatre girl, playing in the band and being made fun of,' she recalled. 'I dressed differently and I came from a different social class from the other girls. I was more of an average schoolgirl with a cork.' A cork that was set to pop with a bang when she left school.

Chapter Four
Graduating From High School – Next Step, NYU

After enduring the oppressive nature of a strict Catholic school for so long, the time for Stefani and her classmates to leave was drawing near. In order to graduate from Sacred Heart, Stefani had to write a thesis on the arts and one on Christianity. She managed to complete them both in time and got top grades as usual. But she couldn't decide what to do when she finished.

She had thought about attending Juilliard, a prestigious dance and drama school in New York with an amazing reputation as one of the top schools for performance arts. Famous acting alumni include Robin Williams, Val Kilmer and Kevin Spacey, while the list of famous musicians that have graduated from Juilliard is as long as Stefani's arm.

Stefani wasn't quite sure she wanted to go there, so she signed up for a weekend pre-college programme that taught talented young musicians who were too young to attend full time, so they could see if they wanted to attend the college. The pre-college programme ran on Saturdays, but it was fearsomely difficult to get into, with tough auditions.

Stefani psyched herself up for her entrance audition, but got really nervous beforehand. She didn't usually get stage fright, but something about Juilliard didn't feel right to her, so instead she decided to go to acting school.

She made the decision to go to New York University's prestigious Tisch School of the Arts. Getting into Tisch was hardly easy – the school would receive thousands of applications for only a handful of spots, so all prospective students had to undergo an artistic review, as well as a gruelling interview process.

Standing on the pavement outside the entrance to Tisch, Stefani took a deep breath. She looked at the decorative columns and the stonework standing between her and one of the most prestigious arts schools in the world. She decided she was going to go in there and nail the audition. She took a deep breath, walked into Tisch and gave it everything she had, and the school was obviously impressed – at seventeen, she became one of only twenty kids to gain early admission to Tisch. Studying there would give Stefani the chance to learn more about music, theatre, and dance – three things she was mad about.

The time finally came for Stefani's graduation from high school. When she had entered the upper school, the nuns gave all the students a ring with a heart , which they wore facing inwards. When she graduated, Stefani stood alongside her classmates and they all turned their rings around, showing that they would take everything they had learned from the school out into the world. If anything, the school had shown Stefani who she *didn't* want to be – now she just had to figure out who she *did* want to be.

Walking into NYU that first late summer morning for registration, Stefani still wasn't sure she had made the right choice picking Tisch over Juilliard. Juilliard was a very prestigious school, but she shouldn't have worried on that front as Tisch had its own impressive list of alumni, including Angelina Jolie, Woody Allen, Anne Hathaway and Selma Blair.

Stefani signed up for her classes and began her studies. The musical theatre programme she was taking taught her a lot more than just musical theatre. She took art history classes, from which she discovered a love of Andy Warhol and other pop artists that was to influence her later performances greatly. In the large echo of the design studio, Stefani took classes in set design, which gave her inspiration for the magnificent sets that she and the Haus of Gaga would later put together for her Fame Ball tour. She learned about creative direction, and what it meant to think about her music as a whole – from clothes she wore, to the visuals on the screen, to the dance moves, to the colour scheme. She learned about writing scenes in plays, and how to act as a character on a stage.

'I would dance for five hours every morning, then an acting or singing class, then studies at night, so I would take an art literature and modern art, all kinds of nerdy stuff that I'm into. But now when I'm being bossy on my videos I know all of the jargon and the terms to use so that I sound like a smart girl instead of a twit,' she says of the knowledge she gained in that time.

The focus on acting actually ended up being better for

Stefani, because so much of what she was later to do was persona related. She described it as self-discovery through acting and sense memory. 'Certain positions and dance moves that I would do would resonate more with me than others,' she later explained. 'Like I suck at ballet, but I was excellent at jazz and theatre.'

Even though her college workload was so heavy, she continued the gruelling after-school regime of playing at open-mic nights all over the city with her band, determined to get her sound heard and loved by the crowds. She played at legendary New York talent-spot, the Bitter End – one of the most famous nightclubs in New York's trendy Greenwich Village. The Bitter End opened in 1961, and had some pretty famous guests grace the stage over the years – music legendaries like Stevie Wonder, Neil Diamond, Bob Dylan and Joni Mitchell had all played the club. Stefani played here as often as she could, and with its dark wooden interior, bathrooms covered in graffiti and sometimes-rowdy clientele, it became a second home for her.

Her talent was also getting her noticed around the halls of campus. She competed in an NYU-wide talent showcase called Ultra Violet Live, which pitted her against students from the rest of the university, which she went on to win. She played in a glam-rock band, and many of her fellow students (and other members of staff) became convinced that she was destined for big things.

She had discovered a new sense of freedom at college, something she attributes to having escaped the strict Catholic school environment. The traditions of cabaret, burlesque and musical theatre that she learned about at NYU had given her ideas that would influence her performances.

But there was something else about being at NYU that

Stefani loved – it had let her creative spirit flourish. 'My given name and the girl I was in high school got suppressed,' she later said as Lady Gaga to Australian newspaper *The Age*. 'It was a really conservative high school. It was all regulation. Gaga was always there, but she was toned down and trying to fit in. Once I got to college, I became who I am now.'

But in spite of everything Stefani wasn't happy at NYU. One day she was getting lunch at Dojo, a Japanese diner near campus, when she started wondering what it was about her life that wasn't sitting right. She loved all the information she was getting about performing – she was soaking it up like a sponge – but she wasn't happy. She realised that perhaps the college environment wasn't giving her what she needed: good, solid experience.

'I loved NYU, but I thought I could teach myself about art better than the school could,' she later told *Elle* magazine. 'I really felt New York was my teacher and that I needed to bite the bullet and go it alone. I wasn't interested in going to frat parties and doing those sorts of collegiate things. I was really interested in the music scene and waitressing and cleaning toilets, or whatever the f*** it was I was doing.'

She worried about upsetting her parents – who had sacrificed so much for her education and supported her throughout her life so far – but she realised she had to be true to herself. College wasn't for her. She didn't want to become famous on a whim or through a talent contest. She wanted to earn her stripes the traditional way, with good old-fashioned hard graft.

'I don't have the same priorities as other people,' she told *Rolling Stone* magazine in 2009 about her decision to drop out and go to work. 'I just don't. I like doing this [music] all the time. It's my passion … When I'm not working I go crazy.'

So the gutsy teenager made the decision to just 'f*** it', as she says in an interview for the website Riffin'. 'I dropped out of NYU, moved out of my parents' house, got my own place and survived on my own. I made music and worked my way from the bottom up. I didn't know somebody, who knew somebody, who knew somebody. If I have any advice to anybody, it's to just do it yourself, and don't waste time trying to get a favour.' It was a decision that would change her life.

Chapter Five Going It Alone: Meet Lady Gaga

Stefani Germanotta thought long and hard, but finally made the decision to drop out of NYU. Just after her nineteenth birthday, she broke the news to her parents, who took it better than she had expected. They were, of course, a little concerned about her decision – NYU was a great university and they worried that if she dropped her studies now, she would never return to them – but they also knew their daughter. Stubborn and headstrong, she never chose the easy path.

'I'm leaving,' she told them, confronting them in typically abrupt fashion. 'I'm going to get an apartment, work eight jobs, and find my own way in the music business.'

Mum Cynthia started crying. But after a brief discussion with her dad Joseph, her parents decided that if this was what she wanted to do, they would support her. However, her father gave her a time limit: she had one year to get signed to a label, otherwise the deal was off and she would have to return to school.

Stefani was ecstatic. Her parents offered to help her financially by paying for her rent, but she was adamant she didn't want to take anything more from them. They had already done so much, and she wanted to prove to them, and to herself, that she could do it on her own. And if that meant making tea, cleaning toilets or sweeping floors, then that's what she would do.

She knew exactly where she wanted to move to – New York's East Village, a trendy neighbourhood that during the 60s had attracted artists and hippies because of the low rents. Many musicians lived in the area, and new venues were opening up all the time, bringing a new wave of music to New York. The East Village's Fillmore East had helped establish British bands like Pink Floyd and Led Zeppelin (two of Stefani's favourites) in America, while another local venue was the infamous CBGB, the birthplace of punk.

The East Village was the starting point for many of Stefani's artistic heroes, including Patti Smith, Madonna, the Ramones and pop artist Andy Warhol, who had promoted a series of shows in the area in 1966. His philosophy and art was starting to make a real impact on Stefani's way of thinking about music and performance. She felt like living in the neighbourhood where so many of her biggest influences had lived, worked, or got their big breaks would be a positive influence on her journey.

She found a small apartment – far from the luxury she was used to at her parents' grand West Side home – but Stefani knew this would be the base from which she would reach great heights. With a tiny Formica kitchen set, small kitchen table and bedroom barely big enough to swing a cat in, it was a far cry from her parents' large uptown pad where she had grown up. The carpet was dirty, there were cracks in the ceiling, and the windows would occasionally rattle. But this tiny box room represented something much more valuable than she would ever find there: it represented the start of walking her own path.

She looked out of the grubby window onto the street below, and saw the vibrant city life beneath her: people dressed so differently here than back where she was from. Women were sassy, and though they might have been dressed in cheap, five dollar shoes and outfits that were bought from a thrift store, they sashayed down the street as if they were runway models at a Lagerfeld show. All the guys were freaking their own individual styles and looks – there were skaters, rave kids, punks, indie, Goths, club kids. Yes, Stefani thought to herself – this was the place she was meant to be.

While she was enjoying the freedom from her parents and from school, Stefani felt as though something else was at work too. 'I realised my father's sister, who'd died at nineteen, had instilled her spirit in me,' she told the Australian paper the *Sunday Herald Sun*. 'She was a painter, a poet and, even though I'd never met her, one of the most important figures in my life growing up. I had a spiritual epiphany that I had to finish her business.'

She spent the summer waitressing at the busy Cornelia Street Café in the heart of Greenwich Village, and working on songs with her band. When it came to recording her music, rather than get someone in to help them, Stefani decided to do it herself.

'I didn't do a commercial release. It was just like records that I put together on my own,' she later said on The Grind. 'It was really short. I demo'd everything and produced it all myself. It wasn't signed to a label, it was just stuff I was doing in New York. That's the kind of girl that I am. I never waited for somebody to hand me something on a silver platter. I was like, "I wanna make a record, OK, so I'll save up my money and buy a four-track tape recorder." I used to just hustle, I'd grind, I'd do whatever I had to do.'

'Whatever she had to do' also involved taking advantage of her time at NYU by sneaking in to record demos using the university's recording facilities.

Her change of neighbourhood and lifestyle also had an affect on the songs she was writing. 'When I got downtown, there were so many f**king songwriters,' she said in an interview with BlogCritics. 'Everybody did the same s**t, superboring. I wanted to do something that was original and fresh.'

Consequently she was writing fewer sweet, syrupy ballads and more piano-heavy solos that sounded like a combination of Otis Redding, Tori Amos, Elton John, Queen and The Beatles. 'That was my favourite, the incredibly theatrical and emotional stuff, where you could really hear her voice,' her friend Lady Starlight said later.

Her band – called SGBand (SG standing for Stefani Germanotta) – played their first full live performance at The Bitter End in October that year, and Stefani decided shortly afterwards that she wanted to record a demo. The five-track demo was called *Words*, and on it Stefani recorded a song she had written and been playing live for a while, a beautiful track that sounded like an early version of 'Brown Eyes' called 'No Floods'.

She set up a MySpace page – calling herself Stefani Music at this point – and started talking to her fans, and telling them where and when she'd be playing next, trying to create a small community and a buzz around her performances.

It seemed to work. Encouraged by the hype, she decided to record and release her first EP, called *Red & Blue*. The EP featured tracks 'Something Crazy', 'Wish You Were Here', 'No Floods', 'Words' and 'Red & Blue'. Her sound was very influenced by her all-time hero, David Bowie, and placed her within the classic singer-songwriter community in the city. She decided to hold the EP launch at her favourite nightspot The Bitter End, in January 2006. The EP was again a huge success, and as luck would have it, it was heard by Bob Lone, who was the National Projects Director of the Songwriters Hall of Fame. He loved the EP and thought she showed great promise, so chose Stefani to be one of nine performers at the 2006 New Songwriters Showcase at New York venue The Cutting Room. As fate would have it, there was someone at the showcase who would go on to be a big part of Stefani's life – Sony producer, Rob Fusari.

As a writer and producer, Rob had enjoyed many major chart successes. He was one of the key figures in the launch of Destiny's Child, co-writing two of group's biggest hits, 'No No No' from their self-titled début album released back in 1998, and 'Bootylicious', from the 2001 album *Survivor*. He had also worked with a diverse range of artists, from classic dance diva Gloria Gaynor to modern pop icons Britney Spears, Will Smith and Jessica Simpson.

Rob, who was born and raised in New Jersey, had a remarkably similar musical childhood to Stefani. He began studying classical piano when he was eight years old, and was such an incredible talent that he was performing in national competitions by the time he was ten. He made it to the finals three years in a row, getting the opportunity to play the legendary Carnegie Hall each time.

He had started writing songs in college, and began collaborating with other songwriters, penning tunes with and for artists of many genres: pop, rock, country, hip-hop, and dance. He moved to LA to pursue his career, but then moved back to New Jersey to set up his own production company, where he'd worked with many skilled artists.

Rob was looking for a new talent and used to visit venues in the East Village whenever he heard that new talent showcases were going on. He knew that you could spot artists that stood out at these events, and he was looking for just that: a diamond in the rough.

Stefani sashayed up the steps and across the stage, set up her equipment and started to sing. From the bar, Fusari turned to look at the stage. He saw a tiny, slender girl with long brown hair sat at the piano with the Macbook booming out beats. There was something about her. He decided to take a chance, and introduced himself to her.

Stefani's style at this point was quite different from the Lady she would later transform into. 'When I started out, I was pretty funky, but not quite so mad,' she says, 'I wore a leotard and had my hair like Amy Winehouse. I would sing and play the piano while wearing a hundred orchids in my hair. I was a real flower child, but quite sweet with it.'

Rob and Stefani started working together at Rob's home studio. The pair got on like a house on fire. He loved her sense of theatre and drama. They wrote a few songs together, which were still in the vein of being ballads. It was around this time while they were working in the studio together that Rob burst out laughing one day at Stefani's theatrics.

'You are just so freaking Freddie Mercury, you're so dramatic!' he laughed. That afternoon he called her Gaga, from the Queen song, 'Radio Ga Ga', and Stefani loved it so much it stuck. The next morning she texted him and told him it was official, he was only to call her Gaga from that moment on.

Her friends thought it was hilarious, but it seemed appropriate; it was as if it had always been her name. Even her mum started calling her Gaga, and she never answered to Stefani again. Finally Gaga had found a name that really reflected her character and who she is; it was her all over.'

As well as finding a name, the music she and Rob were writing was starting to get recognition in the media. Their track 'Wonderful' got Internet radio airplay, hitting a high of number two in the iWebRadio chart.

Gaga, however, was starting to find her music dull. As she tinkled the ivories playing another open-mic night, she looked at the crowd and thought to herself, 'If it wasn't me, I wouldn't listen to this. I would be bored at this show'. She wanted to spice things up a bit, and she started with the music.

Rob Fusari was very encouraging of Gaga's desire to create a more poppy, electro-disco sound. He liked the theatrical side of her performance and told her it didn't matter if she felt like it didn't fit anywhere – someone would come along who understood it and would sign Gaga for her individual style.

The pair named their creative collaboration Team Love Child, since Gaga had described herself to Rob previously as being like the hypothetical lovechild of innovative 70s glam icon David Bowie and master of old time rock'n'roll Jerry Lee Lewis.

Gaga was performing solo now. She would set up her Mac-Book Pro and play acoustic piano with synthetic beats in the background. She also started bringing along a boom box as a prop. But still, she wasn't happy.

As she walked home one night, passing groups of drunk frat boys, strutting transvestites and wasted street kids, she wondered what she could do to her act to spice it up, and make it more interesting for the audience. There were a lot of singer-songwriters hustling the live music circuit in New York – sure, she had a good voice and could play piano, but how did that really make her different? What could she do to make herself stand out from the crowd, and turn her act into something that she would really enjoy too?

Gaga's underground popularity on the New York scene was growing. She was out five nights a week, partying a lot at gay clubs and dive bars, soaking up the atmosphere of the East Village and becoming a part of the scene.

It was around this time that Gaga met her first serious boyfriend. A heavy metal musician called Lüc Carl who, according to *Rolling Stone*, was charismatic and the love of her life. They used to hang around at a joint called St. Jerome's on the Lower East Side's buzzing Rivington Street. It was a dark, stately bar with a DJ, and there was a small stage where a gogo dancer usually performed. This was the spot where Gaga used to end up dancing a lot when she started to gogo.

Lüc would drive Gaga around in an El Camino, and she used to make him dinner in her stilettos and underwear. 'He used to be like, "Baby, you're so sexy!"' she told the *Guardian* in 2009. 'And I'd be like, "Have some meatballs."'

With her love life going well and her musical work going from strength to strength, Gaga became fascinated with 1980s club culture. Consequently, she started working a more dance vibe into her songs, and finally she felt like they were taking shape and becoming something she was excited about. 'It was a natural progression from the glam Bowie-esque, singer-song-writer stuff I'd been working on,' she told *Rolling Stone* in February 2009.

Gaga started listening to classic 1980s bands like The Cure and the Pet Shop Boys, as well as modern bands with a retro 80s flavour, like the Scissor Sisters.

'Oh, I love them, I can't breathe!' she would say later to About.com about her love of the camp popsters. 'I remember the first time I heard them, it was on the radio, and I was like, "Who the heck is that?" They are a big influence. I love the disco, their outfits, and they really care about their performance. Conceptually I just think they're very smart in their approach. I'm also a big Elton John fan, and you can hear his influence on every record, so I love them.'

With Rob Fusari's help, Gaga penned a new song which was nodding to her future dance direction – a song that was heavily influenced by the Scissor Sisters and Prince – a song called 'Beautiful, Dirty, Rich'. She came up with the idea for the song while dancing around her bedroom in her underwear, thinking about her involvement with the arts scene in the East Village, and the kinds of characters she was encountering there; rich kids who ran downtown to escape their families, but who would call their parents to beg for money to go out partying. Later on, Gaga stated: 'That time, and that song, was just me trying to figure things out.'

She elaborated further in an interview with About.com, stating that 'Beautiful, Dirty, Rich' is about a few different things: the idea of inner fame, which was to run through her début album, but also about partying and drug use: 'On the Lower East Side, there were a lot of rich kids who did drugs and said that they were poor artists, so it's also a knock at that. "Daddy I'm so sorry, I'm so, so sorry, yes, we just like to party."

'I used to hear my friends on the phone with their parents, asking for money before they would go buy drugs. So, that was an interesting time for me, but it's funny what came out of that record – because it's about many different things – but ultimately what I want people to take from it is … no matter who you are and where you come from, you can feel beautiful, dirty and rich.'

At the time she wrote 'Beautiful, Dirty, Rich', Gaga was heavily immersed in the kind of life she writes about in the song. 'I was a f**king scenester,' she told Blogcritics in 2008. 'I was partying in a particular lifestyle that everybody lived. It inspired me to try to understand what fame was really all about because we all felt so famous. None of us were. It was because of our love for our work, my love for the music, my love for the fashion, art, culture. Through that, you create an inner fame and I duped a lot of people into thinking I was somebody that I wasn't.'

All the while that Gaga was writing songs on her own and with Rob Fusari, she was constantly performing live, allowing her show to design itself. She had always been interested in the visual elements of other artists' performances, and used the styles of cabaret and burlesque to shape her own.

Always a night owl, she was heavily embroiled in the alternative night-time scene in the city: the dive bars, the club kids, the bands, the brawls, the drink, and the drugs. One night while she was at university, she dropped acid with a group of her friends looking for a spiritual experience. While she was tripping, she hallucinated meeting Thom Yorke, lead singer of

Radiohead and one of her greatest musical heroes. But the odd psychedelic experience here or there wasn't too worrying – lots of her contemporaries at art college were doing the same. But back at home, in her tiny box apartment, things were turning more serious.

In order to achieve the artistic lifestyle that the likes of Andy Warhol and Mick Jagger had led before her, she used to order a bag of cocaine from a delivery service, do some lines, then work on her hair and make-up for hours. She would wake up in the morning at ten-thirty, do some more lines, write music, then stay up for three days in a creative whirlwind of drugs, drink and music.

'I thought I was gonna die,' she said later in an interview with ShockHound. 'I never really did the drugs for the high – it was more the romanticism of Andy Warhol and Mick Jagger and all the artists that I loved. I wanted to be them, and I wanted to live their life, and I wanted to understand the way that they saw things and how they arrived at their art. And I believed the only way I could do this was to live the lifestyle, and so I did. So it wasn't about getting high – it was about being an artist.'

But while she was trying to live the lifestyle of her idols, the reality was harsh. The comedown always hit her hard, and would leave her suffering from panic attacks for a week.

'I wasn't a lazy drug addict,' she told *New York Magazine* in 2009. 'I would make demo tapes and send them around, then I would jump on my bike and pretend to be Lady Gaga's manager. I'd make $300 at work and spend it all on Xeroxes to make posters.'

Although she was getting into a more deviant lifestyle, she was more determined than ever to find that killer opportunity to break into the business. But sometimes getting the right gigs would be difficult. She was still working hard to promote herself – she used to take her demos into clubs, lying to the bar staff and saying she was Lady Gaga's manager, and that Gaga was only available to play on Friday nights at 10:30 – the best time slot. The hustle was starting to pay off, but sometimes she still had to battle for the audience's attention.

Pretending to be her own manager, she hustled herself a Friday night gig at her beloved Bitter End, headline slot, of course. But the show was a disaster. As she hid in a dark corner of the club putting on her fake eyelashes with no mirror, she looked around the audience in horror. Because it was a Friday night, rather than an audience full of her East Village friends (who had actually come to see her play), the venue was full of loud frat kids from NYU, who liked to frequent the venue on the weekends because it didn't ask for ID.

It had been a tough show to set up. And now these horrible frat kids weren't paying any attention to her. Her portable disco ball spun around on the top of the piano next to her MacBook. She caught a million tiny glimpses of her face in it. Failure was not an option. She had to get these kids to listen to her.

And the way she got their attention became a trademark she would later become famous for. She took off her clothes.

Chapter Six
Getting Naked and Getting Signed

To shut the noisy college kids up, she knew she had to do something drastic. She was so angry. She had on a killer outfit that night and knew she was looking totally fly – fishnets, a tight skirt and low-cut shirt. She had some great new material, too, but no way of making them listen to her.

And so she did the only thing she could think of: she pulled off her skirt and took off her shirt. She shook out her long brown hair, which cascaded down her back. And the whole venue – frat kids, East Village misfits, bartenders, everyone – stared at her, wondering what on earth was going on.

'I felt a spontaneity and nerve in myself that I think had been in a coffin for a very long time,' she says. 'At that moment I rose up from the dead.'

Sat at the old battered piano, dressed only in bra, panties, fishnets and white pumps, Gaga carried on playing. Every pair of eyes in the joint was on her. Suddenly people started listening to the music. She had found a way to make the world pay attention, and once she had got their attention, they were hooked on her.

From that moment, something awakened in Gaga. She felt a kind of artistic freedom she had never felt before. All those years of strict religious education and discipline had been great for her report card but had stifled her creatively.

'That's when I made a real decision about the kind of pop artist that I wanted to be,' she later told the *Independent*. 'Because it was a performance art moment there and then … unless you were in the audience in that very spontaneous moment, it doesn't mean anything. It's like, she took her clothes off, so sex sells, right? But in the context of that moment, in that neighbourhood, in front of that audience, I was doing something radical.'

All the way back to her grimy box room apartment that night, she couldn't help but smile. What on earth had made her decide to take her clothes off? She had no idea, but she felt like she was beginning to turn into the person she'd always wanted to be. Stefani Germanotta might never have done that, but Gaga – Lady Gaga – loved doing the unexpected.

As Gaga was becoming more comfortable in her own skin, she was becoming too unconventional for other performance opportunities. She used to audition for stage musicals, hoping to break into Broadway, but the producers wanted a more traditional sound, so they used to reject her, telling her she was too pop for them. And when she auditioned for record labels, they didn't know what to make of her theatrical musical interpretations.

When she turned up for an audition at Virgin Records, an

executive gushed, 'I've read so much about you – apparently you're the talk of the town!' Gaga sat down and played the piano, and by the time the song was finished all eyes in the room were on her. But the exec was shocked: it was so unlike anything he'd heard or seen before. He stared at Gaga with a look on his face that said, 'What *planet* are you from?'

'I took that as such a wonderful compliment, because it was so new to him and so different that he couldn't even wrap his brain around it,' Gaga later told ShockHound. Sick of being told she was too theatrical or too pop, she started wondering whether she should just ignore everyone and do it the way she wanted to do. She thought to herself, 'Well, why don't I do both? And why don't I do it *my way*?' She decided to put all her eggs in one giant basket and just go for it. She never considered a back-up career for a second – there was no alternative.

Despite wanting to spend all her time working on her music, she still had to pay her rent. Working multiple jobs – waitressing at the Cornelia Street Café, bartending at strip clubs – she tried to earn enough money to pay her landlord and support herself while searching for musical fame.

Gaga was also partying harder, going out five nights a week. Drink and drugs were regular features of her nights out, but she didn't feel like she had a problem. She was using them as creative aids, to help her live the lives of her influences, such as Andy Warhol, who had been heavily into drugs.

It was at around this time that Gaga's relationship with Lüc came to an end. The romance was never destined to last and ended badly, hurting Gaga a lot. 'I was his Sandy and he was my Danny, and I just broke,' she explained to *Rolling Stone*. Pretty much all the songs from *The Fame* were inspired by Lüc, and Gaga's relationship with him. Although they remained buddies afterwards, she doesn't like talking about it now, preferring to let the music do the talking for her.

To get over the break-up, Gaga threw herself into her music. But despite working and partying solidly, she decided she wanted more of an insight into the way the music machine operated, an insight she just wasn't getting from her open-mic performances.

She started working as an unpaid intern for Famous Music Publishing, a music publishing division of Paramount Pictures. 'For me, there were no jobs too small, even scrubbing toilets,' she later told *New Times*. Occasionally she would see pop stars like Beck coming in through the doors, and would dream of having a life like his.

Even though she was only working as an intern, Gaga had already adopted the sense of style that she would become famous for, choosing outrageous outfits over the more practical and traditional jeans-and-T-shirt approach. The permanent members of staff were taken aback when Gaga showed up to file papers and sit in on meetings dressed in just a leotard or bra, but they soon realised it wasn't an act or a gimmick when she continued to come to work dressed that way every day.

Jody Gerson, who later signed Gaga's publishing deal with Sony, remembered the youngster's distinctive work uniform: 'Even back then she was famous for showing up for work in her undies!' Jody told *Billboard* magazine in 2009.

The unconventional style of dress that Gaga adopted most of the time, apart from when she was waitressing, also made an appearance when she performed on stage. 'I thought about my fantasy show and wondered, 'What would I be really jealous of if I saw it in New York?' The answer was simple: 'Hot chicks in bikinis!' So Gaga translated this onstage. In general the crowd loved it, though there were some audience members who weren't so keen.

The first time her father watched her onstage, she was dressed in a leopard-print thong fringed bikini, sequinned high-waisted belt and granny panties. Her parents stayed for the entire show, and afterwards her father told her she had done a great job onstage. But he was alarmed and shocked about what he had seen. He could tell by the way she was acting that she was doing drugs, but Gaga was surprised that he knew: 'Because I thought I was slick as fuck,' she explained to the *Guardian*.

She immersed herself in music from the 70s and 80s, wanting to become part of that lifestyle. 'My cocaine soundtrack was always The Cure,' she added to the *Observer*. 'I love all their music, but I listened to this one song ["Never Enough"] on repeat while I did bags and bags of cocaine. "Whatever I do/It's never enough." Isn't that funny? At the time I didn't think there was anything wrong with me, until my friends came over and said, "Are you doing this alone?" Um, yes. Me and my mirror.'

Gaga had made a commitment to her dark side. She wanted to live the lifestyle of the artists she respected – she wanted to know what Jimi Hendrix went through, and how Edie Sedgwick got her look.

Her father wasn't exactly happy about the skimpy outfits and the dancing, but one thing he definitely wouldn't tolerate was drug use. He had played in a bar band when he was younger, and he knew that it was a slippery slope from casual use to addiction. He wasn't about to see his daughter mess up her life like that, or waste her tremendous talent.

Gaga's mum Cynthia told her later that after the show her

father had broken down and confided that he thought their eldest daughter had gone crazy. Later that week, her parents told her, 'It was just really hard to watch that show. We think you've lost your mind and we don't know what to do.'

Her father took her to one side, shaking his head, and said, 'You're f***ing up, kid.'

As she recalled later in an interview with ShockHound, she had no idea how her father knew she was on drugs. 'I looked at him and thought, "How does he know that I'm high right now?" And he never said a word about the drugs, not one word. But he said, "I just wanna tell you that anyone you meet while you're like this, and any friend that you make in the future while you are with this thing, you will lose."'

They never talked about it again, but strong-willed Gaga was able to stop easily, mainly due to a bad experience she had.

'I had a scary experience one night and thought I might die,' she told *The Sunday Times* in 2008. 'I woke up, but it helped me become the person I am. I see things in quite a fragmented, psychotic manner, which I think is because of that. But I decided it was more important to become a centred, critical thinker. That was more powerful than the drug itself.'

She would never fall into that hole again, and the song 'Beautiful, Dirty, Rich' from her album *The Fame* documents this time of her life.

Today, Gaga doesn't like talking about her drug use because she would never want to encourage people to do drugs. 'I kind of feel you're in or you're out with that s***, any hole is deep,' she said to the *Guardian* in 2009.

'I was just being nostalgic and creative and thought that I was Edie Sedgwick and making music. I dunno, I wouldn't necessarily encourage anyone to do it, but I do think that when you struggle, that's when your art gets great.'

So Gaga dropped drugs and the darkness they brought. She didn't attend any rehabilitation classes or therapy. Her father's reaction scared her into realising that she didn't want to mess up her life that way – because that would mean failure, something that Gaga would never accept. She was always an incredibly driven young woman, and her time at Sacred Heart had really drilled into her a fear of failure.

Her father didn't talk to her for months after the incident. Shocked by what he'd seen, he couldn't cope with the thought of his daughter living such a wild lifestyle. But Gaga's mum Cynthia never stopped talking to her daughter. 'Little baby girl,' she told her, 'you can be whatever you want. You are beautiful and you are talented and you could rule the world.'

Although Gaga was upset by her father's response, her mum's support kept her strong and determined that she was on the right path. She focused her creative energies back onto their goal: musical success.

She wouldn't give up on the lifestyle, though, especially not the partying, stripping or provocative dancing. Gaga had found a real personal freedom through her onstage performances, and she was determined to hold onto that.

She didn't need drugs. As long as she was able to express herself creatively she was happy. And she never had any problems taking her clothes off onstage. 'I have a strong sense of my own sexuality. I love the naked human body and I have huge body confidence,' she told *Fabulous* magazine.

Performing like this, Gaga felt like she had found something within her that had always been there, but had been suppressed by years of strict Catholic schooling. 'I've always been Gaga,' she said to *Rolling Stone* in 2009. 'It's just that all the years of schooling and being in a Catholic environment and living in a place where we were kind of told what was the right way to be, I suppressed all those eccentricities about myself so I could fit in.

'Once I was free, I was able to be myself. I pulled her out of me, and I found that all of the things about myself that I so desperately tried to suppress for so many years were the very things that all my art and music friends thought were so lovely about me, so I embraced them.'

By embracing them, Gaga was becoming more comfortable with herself as a performer – and it was beginning to show. Her reputation for strong live performances meant that her shows attracted talent scouts from the record labels. They didn't know what to make of her theatrical performances – sometimes standing on a chair and bending down to play the piano, some-times playing it with her foot as well as her hands. Once again she found herself an outsider, with a style that just didn't fit with the musical pigeonholes that others had created.

Sure enough, a few weeks later, in September 2006, Gaga got a call from a representative at Island Def Jam, a record label group with major acts on its books, such as Bon Jovi, The Killers, and Rihanna. It was a pretty big deal. She turned up to their downtown offices on 8th Avenue, and sang in front of some of the execs there.

The chairman and CEO, Antonio 'L.A.' Reid, wasn't in the room at the time but heard Gaga's huge voice all the way down the hall. She was signed to Island Def Jam there and then and the record label scheduled an album to be released in May 2007.

Gaga was ecstatic, as was Rob when she told him. Finally she would have the backing and support of a major label. She would record a hit album, be number one in America and across the world, and win the hearts of millions of fans. It was her destiny.

Only it didn't go according to plan. In fact, it didn't go anywhere at all. Despite 'L.A.' Reid demanding she be signed to the label, the label didn't know quite what to do with her.

'He took no meetings with me during my stay there,' she later told ShockHound. 'I used to wait outside the doors of his office for hours just to have a meeting with him. And I'd tell my A&R guy "If he's not getting it, I need to talk to him." And he never took a meeting with me, not ever.'

Even the up-beat, hip-hop inspired 'Beautiful, Dirty, Rich' wasn't enough to convince the label execs and she was dropped from Island Def Jam after only three months.

Gaga was devastated. She thought she'd made it, and yet somehow fate had cruelly snatched her life's ambition from right in front of her.

Her father had given her a year to get signed, and she had done it. But it hadn't quite worked out the way she'd hoped. Later, Gaga would look back on her time with Def Jam and the fact that she was dropped, and respectfully say, 'It wasn't for them.'

'We weren't meant to be together,' she said in an interview with Australian newspaper *The Age*, saying of 'L.A.' Reid, 'He's very talented. I don't want to slander him. He signed me, so he has amazing ears.'

It didn't change the fact that she was crushed, though. Many singers in her position would have just given up, thinking it wasn't meant to happen for them.

Her live performances at the time didn't always go so well either. Some nights she would play badly – lose her concentration, miss the right notes or just not give it her all – and she was rewarded by the crowd booing and people telling her she sucked.

But Gaga was stubborn and headstrong, qualities she had inherited from her parents, especially her father, a wealthy self-made man. All her years at Sacred Heart the nuns had taught her that she could do anything she wanted to do; be anything she wanted to be.

She was disappointed, but determined not to give up hope. She knew there had to be something she could do to get back on top. Giving up was not an option.

Meanwhile she worked on more songs with her friend Rob Fusari, determined not to be put off her dream. They started working on an epic pop ballad that would end up as her hit single 'Paparazzi'. The track was inspired by love as well as fame, but it was Gaga's intention that the song would work on a number of levels, allowing people to interpret it in different ways.

'The song is about a few different things,' she later explained to About.com. 'It's about my struggles, do I want fame or do I want love? It's also about wooing the paparazzi to fall in love with me. It's about the media whoring, if you will, watching ersatzes make fools of themselves to their station. It's a love song for the cameras, but it's also a love song about fame or love – can you have both, or can you only have one?' That was a struggle she would face repeatedly and write about for the next few years.

Gaga's and her friends' obsession with fame culture was also encouraged by things she was seeing in the papers on a daily basis. Towards the end of 2006 and 2007, Paris Hilton, Nicole Richie and Lindsay Lohan all started to appear in the papers.

The photographs that were published were mugshots of the young party animals, taken after they'd been arrested for DUI (driving under the influence) offences.

Gaga saw their pouting faces in the tabloids and started thinking the girls were posing – it was as if they were orchestrating being arrested as a publicity stunt. They were playing with the art of fame.

'So much about the youth culture for my generation is celebrity obsession,' she said to The Grind about running with the idea of the art of fame. 'I started to write more records with the art of fame in mind.'

Her fascination with the concept of fame was growing. 'There's something about fame that's taught to us, that it's somehow a validation, when in truth that's not the case at all,' she says.

'I just thought that it was turning into a constant problem,' Gaga said later about what inspired the song. 'So what more important thing to write about than the absolute hugest part of media culture? The paparazzi … I thought about performance art and shock art and how Paris Hilton and her sister and Lindsay Lohan and Nicole Richie are shock artists in their own way. They're not necessarily doing fine arts – something they put in the museums – but it's an art form. That's what this song is trying to say.'

'Paparazzi' would turn out to be Gaga's favourite song on *The Fame*. It was a pop song with ambitions of being a rock opera, and clocked in at way over five minutes long (the average pop song being only three and a half). The charts hadn't heard anything as groundbreaking in pop as Gaga for some years. But there was still a long way to go before she would reach the production of the album as a whole.

She moved apartment from the East Village to trendy Clinton Street on the Lower East Side, hoping that the new location would inspire her. Her new apartment was hardly luxurious – still a box room – and it cost her $1,200 a month, but it was home.

The Lower East Side was a trendy, arty, boho neighbourhood with an endless stream of artists, musicians and scenesters. It was also the location for many of New York's best music venues, bars and clubs. Rivington Street was her base, a popular late-night destination for many of the oddballs and eccentrics that inhabit the New York art scene.

And so, with her new base more deeply rooted in the late-night scene, she returned to the daily grind. Back to the hustle of New York, working her butt off every day, trying to get a break. Luckily for her, that break wasn't far off.

Chapter Seven
Making Good Friends

A bit disheartened but more determined than ever to make it in the music industry, Gaga returned to the hustle of trying to become a pop star in New York. Some would have shied away from the rejection and the gruelling workload, but not Gaga. Music was in her blood, and she knew she had to make it happen for herself.

'Dad comes from New Jersey and he played in bands on the Jersey shore, following in the footsteps of Bruce Springsteen,' she explained to the *Daily Mail*. 'So performing is in my bones and my family instilled in me a ruthless work ethic. I was a pretty fearless chick. No matter how many times I was turned down, I kept coming back.'

Gaga carried on working her three jobs, as well as playing her live shows, just as she had before. She was becoming part of the local scene, meeting more alternative hipsters, artists, musicians and drop-outs in the Lower East Side. There was quite a community in the area, and Gaga loved the vibe – to her, it felt like home.

There was a local metal-glam scene from which she started taking elements she liked and incorporating them into her own style and songwriting. 'The rock star's girlfriend – that was the real beginning of my fashion,' she explains. 'I wanted to be the girlfriend of the lead singer of the greatest rock'n'roll band that ever lived. I wanted to be the girl backstage at the Mötley Crüe concert in the feather dress doing Nikki Sixx's eyeliner.'

Gaga was also obsessed with Versace, Gucci, Dolce & Gabbana, Fendi, Valentino – all the delicious fabric, cuts and silhouettes that she had grown up with, and the fashion sense she had inherited from her well-turned-out mother. Her fashion budget these early days was pretty limited – she would sometimes have no more than five dollars to spend on embellishing or creating an outfit – but she found that no matter what she wore or did, even though nobody knew who she was, she always felt like a million dollars. In her own mind, she was famous already. 'You have the ability to self-proclaim your own fame,' she says. 'You have the ability to experience and feel a certain amount of self worth that comes from a very vain place, by your choices – your opinions about fashion, about music, about politics, the way you walk down the street, the way that you carry yourself at parties – you can literally choose to have fame.'

Gaga learned that you didn't have to be a celebrity or rich or have the paparazzi following you around to be famous: 'Me and my friends just simply declared fame on our own, and we made art and we said, "This is the future" and we dressed in a way that says, "This is fashion".'

Gaga and her artist friends would go out at nights, walking

the streets of New York's Lower East Side like they owned the city. They didn't have any money, they weren't famous, they didn't have paparazzi chasing them, and yet they seemed to attract the attention of everyone who passed them. They glowed with the self-assured aura that only famous people ever seem to possess.

Only they weren't famous. Gaga barely had two dollars to rub together. But it was in this dark and dingy scene – under the crackling neon lights and past the shady-looking guys hanging around in alleyways – that Gaga was the happiest she had ever been in her life.

'That's that inner fame, that's that swagger, that inner sense of passion for your music, and your art, your style, your knowledge about what you do that's infectious. No-one knew who I was but everybody *wanted* to know who I was,' she later said in typically brash fashion to The Grind.

It was this time in her life – feeling like the Queen of the East Village and as if anyone could feel famous – that inspired her début album, *The Fame*.

Gaga's determination was starting to make her new friends. It was at around this time, three months after she'd been dropped by Island Def Jam, that she met the Swedish/Moroccan writer and producer RedOne – Nadir Khayat. RedOne thought Gaga had a real talent.

RedOne had struggled for years before achieving success in the European music industry. The youngest of nine children, at the start of his career he had slept on music studio floors until finally finding success with the group A*Teens and writing the music for the World Cup. Getting to the top of his game in Europe, he'd decided the next move was to conquer America.

The talented producer, who spoke six languages, decided to move to the US, where he started a production company called RedOneKonvict, with singer/songwriter and producer Akon, writing songs for different US acts. He was looking for an artist to work with and decided to take a chance on Lady Gaga.

When the pair met, in late 2006, Gaga was still unsigned and smarting from being dropped by Island Def Jam. She was flat broke, but RedOne thought she was super-talented so worked with her for free.

One of the first songs they worked on together was the infectious dance track 'Boys Boys Boys'. 'I wanted to write the female version of Mötlcy Crüe's "Girls Girls Girls", but with my own twist,' she explains on her website. 'I wanted to write a pop song that rockers would like.'

Later on, Gaga would admit to the *Guardian* that she wrote the song to impress her ex, metal drummer Lüc, who she told *Rolling Stone* was the inspiration for the song.

RedOne helped her realise her vision for the track, which was Gaga through and through – 'gothic pop' as she described it in an interview with DJ Sidekick. With its upbeat tempo and lyrics that referenced rock band The Killers, Gaga loved the new direction her music was taking.

She immediately recognised RedOne as an awesome talent, and learned a lot from him. 'He taught me in his own way – even though he's not a writer, he's a producer – he taught me how to be a better writer, because I started to think about melodies in a different way,' she told About.com.

The track 'Boys Boys Boys' got great reactions whenever she played it live, but soon after they wrote it together, RedOne left New York for a while to work on another project. Gaga continued with her music alone, drawing endlessly on her inspirational surroundings in the Lower East Side.

'Everybody dressed different, everybody talked different, everybody's swagger was different,' she said about the area. Feeling like a part of this artistic community gave Gaga the confidence to experiment more with her music, her style and her look.

During this time she started working with someone who inspired and encouraged her to explore this rock'n'roll part of herself, a rock DJ called Lady Starlight. Gaga had met Starlight through Lüc Carl, who was one of Starlight's best friends, and managed the club she gogo-danced at. But as Gaga's relationship with Lüc started to fade, her friendship with Starlight burned brightly. Gaga was hugely influenced by Starlight. Many years later, when Starlight was asked by Crossfire what her role was in Gaga's global success, Starlight replied, 'My style, performance art and djing inspired her persona. I was also one who told her to take off her pants because I rarely wore any myself.

Starlight – born 23 December 1975 as Colleen Martin – was born and raised in upstate New York. Always into alternative music and lifestyles, Starlight had a degree in philosophy and had lived in London for two years before moving back to New York City in 2001.

Even though she was almost ten years older than Gaga, they were kindred spirits. Starlight was a creative soul who lived her life spontaneously and for one purpose: to express herself through her art.

During the day, she worked to pay the rent as a make-up professional for MAC Cosmetics, but by night she was a rock-'n'roll DJ, promoter and gogo dancer.

'She got me into gogo dancing,' Gaga remembers about the

start of their friendship. 'I thought she looked so amazing on stage, so I thought, I just have to start.'

As Gaga was still flat broke, rather than buy outfits to gogo dance in, she made her costumes herself.

Her look – which she described to *Women's Wear Daily* in mid-2007 as 'filthy, unacceptable' – was achieved by shopping at Manhattan's M&J Trimming, a fabric and trimmings store, from which she would buy tiny stick-on diamanté jewels for her bikinis, or lengths of tassel to sling around her waist. She would also buy leggings from American Apparel.

'I'm somebody that likes to experiment with different things, so I bought a lot of leather and a lot of sequins and started making things,' she says. She used to buy cheap bras and customise them by draping chains over them or attaching tassels.

The practice she got as a child when making her *Billy Goat Gruff* horns, and altering clothing as a teenager came in useful when fashioning clever pieces of stage clothing out of coat hangers and scraps of material. For footwear during her performances, she would buy heels from the stripper shops on 42nd Street, explaining, 'They're made to be more comfortable, so that I can dance onstage but still have the height.'

Her love of artists like Madonna and David Bowie showed in the outfits she made. She loved their innovative visual style almost as much as their music, because the visual aspect changed the way she listened to them, and she wanted to incorporate the same thing into her own stage fashion. 'No one wants to see David Bowie doing Ziggy Stardust in a sweat suit,' she said to *Women's Wear Daily*. It was a mantra she would repeat for years when defending her fashion choices.

Gaga's individual sense of style was everyday wear for her now – she couldn't imagine hanging around in sweatpants or loose vests. Typical daywear for her would be an animal-print bikini, a pink sequined belt, black spandex leggings and Jimmy Choos. 'This is my daywear,' she explained to *Women's Wear Daily* in 2007. 'I'm not comfortable in a T-shirt and jeans.'

Gaga started dancing onstage to tracks by metal bands she loved, such as Metallica, AC/DC and Slayer. She would wear skimpy hand-made costumes that consisted mainly of leather, and carried a portable fog machine in her handbag so she could fog herself onstage. She would hustle at the clubs she danced at, begging the DJs to play her records while striking evocative poses on the stage and dance floor, much to the entertainment of the DJs and the club regulars.

Inspired by the burlesque scene and looking for ways to spice up her performance, she found a small, underground music store in the heart of Brooklyn, where they pressed vinyl dubplates for reggae and dance artists to use.

Gaga had a brilliant plan, which involved her newest creative partner. She would get her pop beats pressed onto vinyl and ask Lady Starlight to play them while she performed and played synthesizer rather than piano, to add a real 80s vibe to her show. Her keyboard, of course, would be lowered, so she had to bend over and show the audience her cleavage.

No one was playing pop records in the underground scene. Pop had become a dirty word in venues and clubs. Instead people would concentrate on 'serious' indie bands and singer songwriters, but Gaga felt that the live music scene was lacking fun and vitality. It also felt like she was breaking a taboo by playing pop records in dive bars and dirty, urine-stained venues with sticky carpets and rowdy audiences.

'It was the most provocative thing I could do in the underground scene,' she said later. 'There's nothing more provocative than taking a genre of music that everybody hates and making it cool.'

So in early 2007, Gaga and Starlight started working on Gaga's new show. They were hanging out together a lot and sharing creative ideas and energy. They would spin vinyl in Gaga's apartment, sewing their bikinis for the show and listening to David Bowie and the New York Dolls, dreaming up ways to make their act the talk of the town. 'At the time, we thought, What could we do to make everybody so jealous?' she said to *New York* magazine in 2009.

As the girls were too poor to pay for rehearsal space, they used to practise in Gaga's apartment. They set up Starlight's turntables in the kitchen, with Gaga on piano and microphones hooked up to an amplifier. They made a lot of noise through this relatively modest set-up, upsetting Gaga's neighbours, who used to bang on the walls shouting at the girls to be quiet.

They rehearsed Gaga's music over and over again, but as Starlight watched her friend sing, she saw something deeper going on. Like her musical idols David Bowie and Grace Jones, Gaga wasn't just singing, she was becoming the music, embodying everything from the lyrics to the beats to the melody.

Starlight stopped the turntables. 'It's not really a concert and it's not really a show. It's performance art,' she said.

'Really?' asked Gaga, unsure of what her friend was getting at.

'Yeah,' answered Starlight. 'What you're doing isn't just singing ... it's art.'

Starlight pointed out that already so much of Gaga's show was different from conventional artists – they were spinning computer-programmed beats on vinyl records no less.

Gaga had never thought of herself as a performance artist until that point. Perhaps that was why the musical producers didn't want to take her on, and why the label bosses didn't know what to make of her. She was bringing something to them that didn't fit their mould, something that was unique and totally Gaga!

They called the act Lady Gaga and the Starlight Revue, and played gigs across New York throughout the spring and summer of 2007. Their first gig was on 24 April at Gaga's favourite haunt, The Bitter End.

Both girls rocked matching styles as they took to the stage. With long, dark brown hair and bangs, Gaga looked more like Amy Winehouse than the brilliant peroxide blonde she would metamorphose into a year later.

Starlight also had long black hair and bangs, and the pair wore matching, daring black cutaway leotards. Gaga wore electric pink fishnets and knee-high boots as she rocked the synthesizer, while Starlight wore black tights and knee-high red boots, spinning beats on her turntables.

The girls danced choreographed gogo routines together, playing with disco balls the size of beach balls, and for their most dangerous party piece, they'd set light to streams of hairspray – sometimes towards the audience.

The show was a hit. With their raunchy outfits, synchronised dancing and Gaga's incredible voice, they created a stir underground. Sell-out crowds turned up to see their shows at New York venues like Rockwood Music Hall and Mercury Lounge. The girls got their biggest gig in July at nightspot Rebel, where they opened for local glam-rock band Semi Precious Weapons. Once again the girls were there to shock. In matching black bra and panties, plus huge see-through plastic heels, and heavy black eyeliner, the crowd couldn't keep their eyes off them.

Gaga had created a reputation for herself far further afield than just New York, though, although she didn't realise it at the time. In early 2007, her creative partner Rob Fusari had sent some of her music to one of his old friends Vincent Herbert.

Rob and Vincent had met in the mid 90s, when Vincent had been working with Destiny's Child and Rob had been a songwriter. They collaborated on Destiny's Child's first hit 'No No No', and after that started working as production partners in LA.

After ten years of LA, though, Rob had had enough. He missed his native New Jersey, so moved home and set up his own production company, but he was still in close contact with Vincent, especially when it came to musical talent as special as Lady Gaga. Nearly a year after he and Gaga met, he sent Vincent some of her songs, determined to get her talent noticed.

Highly impressed, Vincent flew to New York to see Gaga perform live. Rob took his old friend to see Gaga and the Starlight Revue, and Vince was gobsmacked. The lively, kick-ass show, upbeat tunes and sexy outfits brought a shimmer of glamour and fun that had been missing from pop music for some time.

Vince knew he was in the presence of something very special and had no hesitation in signing Gaga to his label – Streamline Records, a part of huge label Interscope – on the spot. She would be part of a new roster of artists at Interscope that had been formed to develop new talent: Cherrytree Records.

Finally, after hundreds and hundreds of live performances, months of working multiple jobs and living on the breadline, it looked like things were moving in the right direction.

Chapter Eight
Playing Lollapalooza

Things were getting better and better for Gaga. She'd been signed to a major label and music industry legend Vince Herbert seemed to understand her talent and creative direction – it felt like a much better move than Island Def Jam and she was confident it would be a fruitful endeavour.

It seemed like things couldn't get any better, and to top it all Gaga and the Starlight Revue were booked to perform at one of America's biggest festivals.

In August 2007, Gaga and Starlight packed up their belongings and headed for Chicago. Neither could believe they were about to perform at one of America's biggest music festivals – Lollapalooza. It was like a dream come true.

Lollapalooza was set up in 1991 as a farewell tour for the alternative rock band Jane's Addiction, but continued running every year until 1997. It was revived in 2003, and became one of the most important and popular festivals in the US.

The line-ups for Lollapalooza covered mainly alternative rock, hip hop and punk rock bands, as well as dance and comedy performances. The festival was widely accepted as being the breaking ground for alternative rock bands to gain widespread popularity. Bands that have successfully played Lollapalooza in this way are Pearl Jam, The Smashing Pumpkins and the Red Hot Chili Peppers.

Lollapalooza's crowd were seasoned indie/rock veterans and Gaga and the Starlight Revue were quite different to the other acts on 2007's bill, which included Daft Punk, Yeah Yeah Yeahs, Snow Patrol, Kings of Leon and The Cribs. The last thing the audiences would be expecting were two hot chicks in bikinis dancing to pop onstage. But Gaga couldn't wait to see what reaction they'd get.

In honour of the big occasion, Gaga had made herself a bikini top covered in mirrors, inspired by late glam-rock king, Marc Bolan, one of Starlight's biggest musical heroes. The idea, she said later, was to make her boobs look like two disco balls. That, and the mirror trim she added to her pants, made her look very disco indeed.

The festival, held at Grant Park in Chicago, attracted nearly 60,000 music lovers in 2007, though it's unlikely that any of them had heard of the gutsy New York girls Gaga and Starlight. On Friday 3 August, the opening night of the festival featured artists and bands like M.I.A., LCD Soundsystem and Electric Six. It was an insanely hot day, and people in the crowd were emptying bottles of water over themselves to cool off.

Starlight and Gaga watched from the audience; they could barely believe that the next day they would be on stage, singing and performing in front of the huge crowd of people.

When Saturday came, Gaga and Starlight stood in the wings, getting ready to go out. There was a huge crowd waiting to see them, and although rain swept in later, the sun shone for Gaga and the Starlight Revue.

The girls took to the stage, Gaga wearing a sparkly blue dress and Starlight an Iron Maiden denim vest. Although they were covered up, both girls wore killer five-inch heels, signalling to the audience that this would be a performance unlike any other they would see that weekend.

A giant disco ball was lowered into the middle of the stage and the two 'Ladies' stood with their arms frozen in the air while Gaga's trusty fog machine created some atmosphere around them. Gaga went to her synths and Starlight to her turntables, then the pair danced and stripped down to their underwear in front of the audience. At least that part of the routine went according to plan, and the dancing – provocative gogo-dance turns set to killer pop choruses – went down a storm.

Between songs, the girls sprayed their long locks with hairspray, before setting streams of it on fire, a trick they'd brought with them from the dark clubs of New York.

The audience were totally shocked. They weren't expecting to see anything like this at an alternative music festival. Mesmerized by the two hot chicks stripping, dancing, spraying fire and playing pop music, they began to cheer and clap.

But not everything went according to plan. The pair experienced tremendous technical difficulties on stage, and Gaga found it nerve-racking trying to get through their equipment problems in front of such a big audience. She hadn't faced anything this big before; it was very different from the seedy, dark, urine-stinking dive bars she performed in back home.

With nerves of steel, Gaga managed to get through the set of nine, synth-driven pop songs she had written, including the unreleased 'Blueberry Kisses' and 'Dirty Ice Cream', and tracks that would make it onto her début album, *The Fame*: 'Boys Boys Boys', 'Beautiful, Dirty, Rich' and 'Disco Heaven'.

'That was not a performance that I choose to remember so fondly,' she said afterwards to About.com. 'But if anything, what I loved the most about it was that the sea of hippies and so forth that were there were not expecting what they saw and I loved the shock art aspect of it.'

Although she might not remember the performance fondly, the reviews and blogs went wild for her after the festival. 'Lady Gaga – What the hell did I just witness? Amazing!' wrote one reviewer.

The shock aspect of performing was definitely beginning to appeal more and more to Gaga, and she was becoming fascinated by it. 'The audience must've thought "Who is she? Why is she here? And is this even music?" And I loved that,' she said. 'I inspire shock in people, and it's fascinating to me. What's so shocking? I just want people to be entertained in a way that they're not used to, and you'll never see the same show twice.'

Although Gaga and Starlight felt their show could have gone better, they were upbeat and decided to spend the rest of the day celebrating their performance. But this wasn't to go without incident when Gaga had a run-in with the police. It wasn't the typical, party-fuelled drugs bust you might have expected, though, rather, Gaga's tiny hot pants over her spandex leggings and knee-high boots proved too much for one bicycle-bound policeman.

'You need to put your ass up against the fence,' the officer told her. 'There are children around here.'

Gaga was incredulous. She could wander around her Lower East Side neighbourhood dressed in hot pants, six-inch heels and leopard-print tank tops, yet here at a music festival in Chicago she was being arrested because of her outfit?

She spoke to *Women's Wear Daily* after the weekend. 'There's a huge festival with people doing cocaine and marijuana, and he's busting me?' Never without her dry, New York sense of humour, she added, 'I really wanted to get cuffed in a jump-suit.'

As if the technical difficulties onstage and the hot-pant incident weren't enough, Gaga also faced problems with the paparazzi that weekend, although for a very different reason to the ones she would have hoped for.

Pop singer Amy Winehouse was also performing at Lollapalooza that weekend, on the Bud Light stage, and with their slender frames, tattoos and long dark hair, you could see how perhaps, from a distance, some lazy journalists and photographers who hadn't done their research properly might mistake Gaga for the British pop minstrel.

For Gaga, though, although it attracted media attention, it wasn't the kind she'd been hoping for. Paps chased her around all weekend, calling, 'Amy! Amy!' and one journalist spent five minutes speaking to her before realising she wasn't the British singer.

After getting back to New York, Gaga and the Starlight Revue played another couple of shows, including the Extreme Hangover, Labour Day Edition at the Cyn Lounge. For this performance the girls made a short video for the Internet advertising the gig, which showed them gyrating and dancing onstage in bikinis while a noisy Metallica soundtrack played in the background.

Gaga bought some peroxide and bleached her hair into a shocking mess of blonde, channelling an early-80s Madonna. 'Amy is a badass but I want to be known for my own look,' Gaga later explained to the *Sun* newspaper about her decision to change her style drastically.

She débuted her new blonde look at a party that she and Starlight put together, called the New York Street Revival and Trash Dance. Described on the flyers as 'burlesque pop, rock'n'roll, glam, metal', the show was designed to run for the first three Thursdays throughout October, and was held at the Slipper Room.

The show also had a slightly different stage concept. As well as Gaga and Starlight onstage, there would be two backing dancers to do routines with Gaga while Starlight played the backing tracks on vinyl.

The shows were a great success, but Gaga's new style and performance came as quite a shock to those who had known her as Stefani Germanotta.

'I was so shocked when I first saw her perform as Lady Gaga,' said Cristina Civetta, the New York writer and fashion designer who had gone to Sacred Heart with her a few years earlier. 'It was at a Lower East Side club, The Slipper Room, and she was in a coned bra and little hot pants. I said, "Damn, you have changed!"

'But when we got to talking, she hadn't changed at all. She wasn't even drinking. She was still one of the nice girls. I really think her morals are still intact,' Cristina added, speaking to the *Daily Mail* in March 2009.

Though her live performances might have been shocking

for those who had known her before, Gaga was exactly the same girl she'd always been. Raised by her parents to be hard-working, respectful and ambitious, she still had all those qualities. Only now the experimental side of her that had lay dormant for so long had been unleashed – and it was wearing hot pants.

The October performances of the New York Street Revival and Trash Dance were a hit on the Lower East Side. But little did Gaga know that forces were at work, far away from the dirty dive bars scene of underground New York, forces that would move her career on to its next level.

Chapter Nine
Akon Offers a Hand

Although RedOne and Gaga had only managed to work together for a short while, RedOne was blown away by her. She had a great ear for a pop song, and he knew she would be the perfect addition to his side project – music production company RedOneKonvict – which he ran with Akon.

Urban music writer, producer and performer Akon was born as Aliaune Thiam in Dakar, Senegal, as the son of a jazz percussionist, according to the *NME*. After spending his youth in Africa, Akon's family moved to America, settling in New Jersey. When he was in high school he got into trouble with the police, but serving time in jail made the teenager determined to turn his life around and follow his father into the music business.

When he was released, he recorded a demo tape, which he sent to major label Universal, who offered the youngster a contract. At this point he took the name Akon (actually his middle name) to mark officially the beginning of his music career, and recorded his début album, which was a big hit.

Having inherited the talent for writing and performing music from his father, Akon set up a number of side projects, including an organisation to rehabilitate prisoners after they're released from jail, and launching his own record label, Konvict Muzik. RedOneKonvict – another side project – was set up with RedOne to write music for established artists such as New Kids on the Block and Brandy.

Akon remembers how persistent his production partner was about getting Gaga onboard. 'RedOne kept blasting me: "Gaga, Gaga, Gaga!" At the time I really didn't understand, but we were working on the Pussycat Dolls and we brought her in to do some writing for us,' he told the *B96 Morning Show*.

Gaga couldn't believe it. She was over the moon to be offered a chance like that. Although she was still focused on gaining musical recognition for performing her own music, it was an opportunity to work alongside established creative minds. She jumped at the chance, but in her own mind she was doubtful about whether she'd fit in with these established music industry types.

For their first meeting, Gaga couldn't help but be nervous and doubt her abilities. 'I was just thinking, "What the hell does this guy see in me?" I'm just like a downtown New York chick, kind of nerdy. I just didn't know that he would think I was fly. But he did!' she says.

For Akon, it was only a matter of days before he realised the extent of Gaga's talent. After they started working together writing songs, he realised 'how dope she was as a writer. Then the next day she was demoing out doing some vocals, and I realised how dope she was as a vocalist. Then the next day I was like, What is she gonna wear today!?

'And everyday she was wearing something new, different, colourful and so 1980s. It was like, this is just her. She wasn't programmed to do it, it's just her,' he said.

In Akon's opinion, having the kooky dress sense wasn't as important as being a good vocalist, but it showed him that Gaga was already channelling her inner superstar. 'It shows you that the artist has already identified who they are, so it makes it easier for you – you don't have to "image" them. They're already exactly what you see,' Akon explained on *B96*.

Gaga's talent as a songwriter and vocalist, and her sense of her own style, meant only one thing to Akon, and he could see it a mile off: sure-fire star quality. Something that, in his long experience in the music industry, was extremely rare.

She had also had a lot of experience. Admittedly it wasn't at such a high-profile level, but her years of hustling in New York – writing music, playing shows constantly, interning at record labels and her encounters with the darker side of the party lifestyle – had taught her valuable lessons about the music business.

She knew to keep her head clean from the distracting influence of drugs. She knew that she wanted to be surrounded by her intelligent, creative, artistic friends, who encouraged her to be herself and helped her realise her musical visions. Sacred Heart had taught her that failure was not an option, while her vocal coach Don Lawrence had instilled in her a sense of hard work and discipline. She had started to gain recognition for her work once she'd embraced who she really was – an off-the-wall performer, who liked to think of her songs as performance art, not just pop records. Being true to herself was the most important thing in the world, and that was never going to change. These were all lessons she never could have learned if she had become famous for winning *American Idol* or some other talent contest.

Gaga was so driven and ambitious, she used to worry about taking time out of her day to sleep. But she stopped worrying about that soon after she met Akon, who, she soon realised, had an even tougher work ethic than she did.

'He for real doesn't sleep,' she told *B96*. 'I've been in the studio with him until five or six o'clock in the morning, and his manager will walk in and be like, "You've got an 8a.m. TV performance". He's like, "OK, just another thirty minutes." Then he'll go do it, then go back to the studio all day. He doesn't stop. I used to worry about sleeping, but now I don't any more!'

Although she was amazed by Akon's stamina, in his mind, he was doing no more than what he'd signed up to do when he launched his label.

'People forget that this is a job,' he says about working in the music industry. 'You know how this is so fun, there are so many advantages that come with it that you forget that you're actually working. That happens a lot.'

One girl it wasn't going to happen to was Gaga. She started working in the studio with Akon on tracks for the forthcoming Pussycat Dolls album, *Doll Domination*, penning tracks with experienced industry writers like Fernando Garibay and Rodney Jerkins.

Jerkins was an experienced songwriter, having penned numerous hits for a variety of artists since 1994. He had run a couple of record labels and was head of A&R at Island Def Jam, the label that dropped Gaga only months earlier, though neither was bitter about working with the other. Gaga had been very gracious about being dropped by the label and was incredibly happy with the way things had turned out instead.

Gaga and Jerkins worked on a couple of songs together for the Pussycat Dolls. They finished one song in the studio, which didn't quite fit the Dolls' sound, but Gaga loved it so much she decided to sing it herself.

The next day, Rodney was in the studio listening back to the recording they'd made of a track called 'Quicksand' when Larry Rudolph, Britney Spears' manager, popped in to say hello.

He heard the music and freaked out. 'Who the hell is this?' he demanded. 'Britney's gotta sing this!'

Jerkins was confused. Britney had been in the media a lot at the time. There were pictures on the Internet of her allegedly under the influence of drugs, the media were saying she was having a breakdown and reporting that the courts were going to take her kids away from her. Jerkins didn't realize that despite all that, Britney was still looking for songs to sing. Rudolph confirmed that Britney was doing a new album and begged to take the song for her to listen to.

Jerkins called Gaga later with the news, saying, 'Britney's people are freaking out about this song!'

Gaga was ecstatic. She'd been a huge Britney fan, and couldn't believe that one of her music heroes might actually like a song she had written enough to sing it herself!

Even though Britney's manager loved the song, Gaga knew that the decision would come down to Britney herself. It was a nail biting few days before she and Jerkins heard from Rudolph again, who called them to say that Britney loved the song and was going to record it.

'When I found out that she loved it and was going to record it, it was amazing,' Gaga gushed happily. She remembered fondly the times when she was in middle school, when she and her girlfriends would take the bus to *TRL* after school and scream for Britney in Times Square. She remembered how Britney and all the other Mickey Mouse Club kids would cause traffic jams as riots of screaming teenagers blocked the streets.

Gaga became more determined than ever to reach her goal of musical fame. She wanted to cause traffic jams of her own – nothing less would do.

Gaga found the songwriting process for other artists came easily and always wrote big, melodic choruses into her songs. She would write mostly at the piano, and often joked that she would do her best work when she was f***ed up – hungover and tired. For Gaga, songwriting was a quick process. 'A hit record writes itself,' she told *Billboard*. 'If you have to wait, maybe the song isn't there. Once you tap into the soul, the song begins to write itself. And I usually write the choruses first, because without a good chorus, who really gives a f***?'

Gaga's time limit for beginning to work on a song was half an hour. If it took longer than that then, in her opinion, it probably wasn't a good song anyway.

Her approach to songwriting was refreshing for industry heavyweights like Rodney Jerkins, who had written hits for huge names like Brandy and Monica ('The Boy Is Mine'), Michael Jackson ('You Rock My World'), Whitney Houston ('It's Not Right But It's Okay'), Destiny's Child ('Say My Name') and Beyoncé ('Déjà Vu').

Jerkins had worked in the industry for a long time and collaborated with many songwriters and producers in his time. So he was surprised with Gaga's professionalism and talent as a songwriter, especially considering she was only twenty-one years of age. She used a slightly different approach to writing songs for other people than she did when writing for herself.

'Sometimes when I do something for myself I'll be a little bit more risk-taking,' she explained to *iProng* magazine. 'I'll just think about something that I could maybe handle that nobody else could. But I pretty much approach them the same way. Writing a pop song and a big chorus, it's special for each song. Sometimes I'll tailor-make something for a particular artist and use them as my muse, but in terms of melody and stuff I always sort of come from the same soul place.'

As well as working on specific projects for Akon, Gaga became his creative sounding board for lyrics and melodies. He credited her with being able to break through any creative mental block he had. The pair built up a close working relationship, which Gaga remains notoriously close-mouthed about to the media, preferring to keep their creative partnership private, although she has stated a number of times that she became a much better songwriter after working with Akon.

'Akon is a very talented songwriter to work with,' she said to About.com. 'His melodies, they're just insane. It's funny, I think about him a lot when I'm doing my melodies because he's so simple, and he's just been great.

'He keeps me on my feet, very grounded, but he also puts me on a silver platter, which is always very nice. So it's been an incredible influence. It's like every time you work with somebody that's better than you are, you become greater.'

Outside the studio, Akon was very supportive of Gaga's personal work as an artist. Even though his label, Kon Live Distribution, was predominantly for R&B and hip-hop acts, there was a quality to Gaga's music that he felt was universal.

Everyone who saw her show seemed to connect with her – girl, boy, gay, straight, urban, rock, indie, dance, pop – so Akon decided to take his support to another level and sign her as an artist to his label.

Gaga was already signed to Vince Herbert's Streamline Records, which might have made things difficult, but both Streamline and Kon Live are part of the mega-label Interscope, so effectively Vince Herbert and Akon had the same boss: Interscope overlord and chairman Jimmy Iovine.

Luckily for all parties concerned, Jimmy had no problem with the deal. He was a big fan of Gaga's. In fact, the pair got on like a house on fire. 'I'm the kind of Italian Brooklyn girl he would have liked to take to the prom,' she laughed, talking to the *LA Times* music blog. 'He *loves* me.'

After extensive talks with Vince Herbert and Jimmy Iovine, the deal was done. From having no record label a few months earlier, suddenly Gaga was signed to three: Streamline, Kon Live and Interscope, an arrangement she described as 'the dynasty'.

As 2007 drew to a close, Vincent Herbert was also talking to Gaga about writing songs, but not for other people. He wanted her to start work on her début album, but for that, she was going to have to make a drastic change to her life. She was going to have to leave the city she loved, the home that had inspired her so much, and move to Los Angeles in California – right over the other side of the United States.

Although she already had some tracks like 'Beautiful, Dirty, Rich' penned for her album, she knew she needed some more hits before she'd be happy with it.

It was a sad time, knowing that she was going to be leaving her friends in New York. She was happy to be working on her music full time, but a little part of her was sad to be leaving the hustle and bustle of her home city.

To celebrate her success, on New Year's Eve 2007, Gaga, Lady Starlight and their friend Darian Darling hit the town. Gaga was still rocking her blonde hair, though it was more of a dirty blonde at this point, and she wore a black dress with black heels. Darian and Lady Starlight both wore heels and white fur coats, and the friends had a fabulous evening. Gaga decided that wasn't a good enough way to say goodbye to her friends, though, so she arranged a farewell party at a bar her friends always drank at on Rivington Street.

Gaga invited all her friends from the Lower East Side, and being in a crazy mood she decided to take all her luggage to the bar with her, so she could go straight to the airport for her early-morning flight to Los Angeles. She didn't want to waste a second with her beloved friends. And it was a wild party – one that would be well remembered in the history of Lady Gaga.

Chapter Ten
Moving to LA

Gaga's wild farewell party was still going strong in the early hours of the morning when the car arrived to take her to the airport. She had been happily drinking her favourite – red wine – all night, and as a result the party had got a little out of hand.

She'd partied with her shirt off for most of the night, so when the car arrived she had to quickly cover herself up, grab her bags and blow kisses to all her friends. Somewhere in the bar she'd misplaced her keys (though she didn't need them, of course: she was heading to a brand-new apartment in Los Angeles) and phone.

Having celebrated heavily all night, Gaga suffered a terrible hangover during the five-hour flight. She flicked through the music on her iPod to distract her from how bad she felt, and decided to listen to an old favourite, The Beatles' album *Abbey*

Road. 'Whether you can hear it or not I was listening to *Abbey Road* … on repeat while I was making this album,' she said later about how other artists' music had influenced *The Fame.* 'I think mostly the joy in that record, the melody line, the celebration.'

When the plane landed she was still hungover, but ever-determined Gaga went straight to the studio to get to work 'in a hungover fit of "I need to write a hit record"', she said later to *B96.* 'I wrote "Just Dance" with my shirt inside out. And I had no keys or phone!'

The studio she was due to record in was the famous Record Plant, one of the most famous recording studios in America, and the place where some of her favourite artists, such as Queen and Black Sabbath, had recorded many of their albums.

Gaga was awestruck when she got there. 'Record Plant is one of the biggest most amazing studios ever,' she said. 'It was so different for me as someone who was always working out of my apartment or home studios – you walk in and Kanye's mixing his record, Snoop Dogg's down the hall, Teddy Riley's there.'

Luckily for Gaga, there was an old friend at the Record Plant waiting to greet her with a big smile on his face. It was RedOne, who she had worked with on the poppy 'Boys Boys Boys', and who had demanded that his production partner Akon start working with her.

She was delighted to see him and so excited to be in the studio. 'I felt like I was Madonna in 1985, I was like, "Oh my God, this is so huge!"' Gaga remembered afterwards. Her co-managers Troy Carter and Leah Landon were also on hand to welcome her to Los Angeles and the Record Plant. It wasn't long before Gaga started wishing she had taken it slightly easier the night before.

The set-up at the Record Plant was very professional and Gaga wasn't used to being waited on while she worked on her music. Staff would come into the room asking her if she wanted something to drink – she couldn't believe how different it was to recording on a four-track tape recorder in her East Village apartment.

The studio that had been booked out for Gaga and RedOne to use was beautiful and full of amazing, state-of-the-art equipment that blew Gaga's mind. She thought it was so fabulous she hopped around the room, taking pictures with her camera to show everyone back in New York. Apart from sneaking into the recording studios at NYU to use the equipment there, she had never had so much expensive technology at her disposal.

Having learned to do things without any money meant that Gaga was more than happy to use her laptop. And when working with RedOne, the pair of them would make the actual music – i.e. program the beats – on their Apple MacBook Pros. She laughed at how funny they looked, sitting in the corner of the huge studio with all this equipment just using their laptops instead.

RedOne saw how hungover Gaga was and laughed. She was always a party animal, so he wasn't surprised. 'You feel no good!' he said to her.

'I know,' she answered him. 'I had a little bit too much last night.'

RedOne suddenly looked at her. 'Gagi-neti!' he said in his pan-European accent, using his nickname for her. 'I've got an idea…'

And with that RedOne started playing the chords that later formed the body of 'Just Dance'. Gaga loved what she was hearing and started singing, 'I've had a little bit too much...'

'We started singing together, doing the melodies together,' said RedOne. 'She comes up with the lyrics – unbelievable, psycho, sophisticated lyricist that she is. It's not over-thought. It's just 100 per cent inspiration.'

They nearly had the whole track down within twenty minutes. Gaga felt a bit nervous. Her new manager Troy Carter was in the room – she didn't usually allow anyone in the same room as her when she was writing, but she felt like she couldn't say no to him as he was new. Troy couldn't believe what he was hearing – the song was a sure-fire hit and they'd written it in under an hour!

'Then Vincent Herbert walks in. He's like, "Oh my god, that's it!"' says Gaga. 'Then Leah Landon came in – she's my other manager – and she was like, "Play that dance one, I wanna hear that dance one!" It was instant! Everybody went crazy!'

After refining the lyrics and working on the beats, Gaga knew that in writing 'Just Dance' she had created a special kind of magic that would run throughout her début album, *The Fame*. It was a song inspired by a lot of late nights and her friends in New York – things that were dear to her heart.

'The song is really an ode to New York and being out in the clubs, getting too drunk and you really should go home, but instead of going home you just dance through it and get yourself through the night,' she explained to *iProng* magazine.

'But I think on a deeper level, the song is about pushing through in general. I was at a time in my life when I was writing record after record after record, looking for that undeniable first single, and "Just Dance" was my hit.'

Gaga was worried about what Akon would think of it. 'Akon is like the most worldly, cultured … hip-hop, R&B guy … I was like, I don't know what he's gonna think of it.' But she needn't have worried. Akon loved the track so much he lent his talents to producing it with RedOne and Gaga. He also did additional vocals, and even got one of his Konvict acts, Colby O'Donis, to perform on it for Gaga.

Gaga couldn't believe how quickly she had managed to write 'Just Dance'. She had been working on her album back in New York for so long, she felt like she had reached a crossroads with her writing.

'I was trying to be so cool with my own music, but I would get better responses when I would write for other artists because I wasn't trying to be cool,' she told *HX* magazine. 'So when I did "Just Dance" that was my way of being like, "just f***ing write a good song. Stop worrying about what's going to fly in the underground. Worry about writing a great record." Actually, that record ended up being more powerful than any of the songs that I racked my brain writing, and after that it was an influx of record after record. It was almost like a switch went off in my brain, and I figured out how to write a good pop song.'

Recording the album may have been going really well, but Gaga was homesick for New York. 'What am I supposed to do, canoodle with celebrities at a nightclub, with a lemon-drop Midori in my hand? It's not the same as being in a bar that smells like urine with all your really smart New York friends,' she said to *New York* magazine in 2009 about living in Los Angeles.

Luckily for her, working on the album was taking up a lot

of her time, and writing it helped her homesickness. 'I write about what I know,' she told *Elle* about her creative process. 'Sex, pornography, art, fame obsession, drugs and alcohol. I mean, why would anyone care to listen to me if I wasn't an expert in what I write about?

'The album itself is the story of me and my friends, and our lives in New York – and you either want to know about it and be a part of it or you don't. I am completely 100 per cent honest in what I do and who I am, and I've got nothing to hide.'

Gaga was definitely busy, but not so busy that she couldn't meet new, creative friends – friends who would end up forming part of the mythical Haus of Gaga. The Haus was a group of artists, designers and creatives who travelled with Gaga on tour and helped her realise her musical visions, design her clothes and sets and be sounding boards for ideas for the live shows.

One of the first official members of the Haus was the DJ Nick Dresti, whose stage name is Space Cowboy. Born in Paris, he moved to the UK when he was ten and quickly got bitten by the music bug. As a teenager he was DJing in sweaty London clubs, mixing rock with techno, electro, hip hop and straight-up dance.

Space Cowboy had released two albums, but it was a single called 'My Egyptian Lover' that received major daytime play from Radio 1 and other British radio stations. Cherrytree Records kept its eye on what was coming out of the UK – a hotbed of talent when it comes to writers and producers – and they liked what they heard of Space Cowboy's musical style, so signed him in mid 2007.

The label wanted to introduce Gaga to Space Cowboy, thinking they would be dynamite if they could work on some material together. When they spoke they discovered a mutual eclectic love of music.

'I remember our first conversation was on the phone,' Space Cowboy said. 'She was talking about sequins, disco balls, Prince, David Bowie and body paint. Basically, she was speaking my language.'

As the pair hit it off so well on the phone, they decided to meet in person. Space Cowboy finally made it to LA, and he and Gaga got on so well she decided to invite him to join her on the road. Gaga had a pretty small touring ensemble, which at the time consisted only of herself, her managers and two backing dancers, Dina and Pepper.

With a live show in the making, Gaga threw herself into writing the rest of the album. Tracks like 'Again Again', 'Disco Heaven', 'Brown Eyes', 'Beautiful, Dirty, Rich' and 'Paparazzi' had been written with Rob Fusari, the New Jersey producer who'd spotted her in 2006. But she still had more hits to write, and with a new set of creative partners. Gaga and RedOne headed back into the studio to work on the next hit, 'Poker Face'.

'I've dated a lot of guys that are really into sex and booze and gambling, so I wanted to write a record that my boyfriends would like,' Gaga explained to Pop Tarts. 'But something I don't really talk about is if you listen to the chorus I say, "he's got me like nobody," then, "She's got me like nobody." It's got an undertone of confusion about love and sex.'

To add to the song's already risqué lyrics, Gaga used a line from a song she'd written years before in New York called 'Blueberry Kisses', which she had performed at Lollapalooza with Lady Starlight. 'Blueberry Kisses' was about 'a girl singing to her boyfriend about how she wants him to go down on her', Gaga explained later. 'I used the lyric, "Blueberry kisses, the muffin man misses them kisses."' She turned the line into 'I'm bluffin' with my muffin', a lyric that would cause controversy when the song was released as a single.

'Obviously, it's my pussy's poker face!' she would later say on numerous occasions, explaining that the song was about her being with her boyfriend, but fantasizing about being with a woman.

When writing 'Poker Face' – as with all her songs – Gaga kept visual elements of the song in mind for her performances.

'I always have a vision,' she told the *Guardian*. 'When I'm writing a song I'm always thinking about the clothes and the way I'm going to sing … How I move, that kind of stuff is written into the song. It's not just a song, and I'm not just gonna stand on stage and sing.'

She had become interested in art from a young age, and while writing each song, she would imagine a specific shape for it and the performances. 'It's what people remember about icons,' she explained to *ASOS* magazine.

'When I think about David Bowie, I imagine a specific shape – it's his hair from *Ziggy Stardust*. With Grace Jones, I see a shape for her. It's about creating these kinds of shapes for my own work and balancing every outfit like it's a painting.'

More cryptically, when she was being interviewed in Singapore in 2009, she alluded to this visual element of her writing, saying, 'When I write songs I hear melodies and I hear lyrics but I also see colours; I see sound like a wall of colours. For example, "Poker Face" is a deep amber colour, when you see the show you will see that colour.'

Whether her co-producers visualized music in quite the same way is unsure. But one thing is certain, they were all astounded at the professionalism and speed at which she worked.

'She wrote almost all her hits in a week,' said Vince Herbert, who'd signed Gaga to Streamline Records, in an interview with *Billboard*. 'She flew to L.A. and sat in a studio with RedOne and just cranked it out.'

RedOne knew that his love of 80s music was the perfect sound to draw on for making tracks with Gaga. His partnership with her would produce futuristic, aggressive snyth sounds that had been popular in the European dance scene for a long time, but hadn't seen major chart success in America since the 80s.

'I love 1980s music,' RedOne said to Pop & Hiss. 'It's all about emotions, and the chorus elevates you. If you look back in three years, and you look at the hits, they all have the same things. They have a verse, a pre-chorus and a chorus – one that's dynamic and elevates you. You need to make people go crazy when the chorus comes. That's so important on every song with Gaga.'

Gaga was so grateful to the Moroccan producer for taking a chance on her early on: 'RedOne is like the heart and soul of my universe,' she said to About.com. 'I met him and he completely, one hundred and fifty thousand percent wrapped his arms around my talent, and it was like we needed to work together. He has been a pioneer for the Haus of Gaga and his influence on me has been tremendous. I really couldn't have done it without him.'

The president of Cherrytree Records, Martin Kierszenbaum also did some writing with Gaga on *The Fame*, and was impressed with her work ethic. 'She is very focused and very fast,' he said in an interview with *Billboard*. 'She doesn't like to sit around and waste time. When we tracked *The Fame* she sang everything in one take and spent about five hours on the harmony.'

It had been Martin Kierszenbaum who originally introduced Gaga to Space Cowboy. The three of them worked together with Tramar Dillard – better known by his stage name of Flo Rida – on the track 'Starstruck'.

The heavy bass, sharp synths and duet vocals on 'Starstruck' were all the contribution of Space Cowboy, and Lady Gaga later commented that the song was what it would sound like if she and Space Cowboy had a baby.

Gaga was interested in collaborating with other artists too, and the UK was a hotbed of talent she regularly looked to for inspiration. Scottish DJ and producer Calvin Harris, who had hit the charts with his track 'Acceptable in the 80s', was someone Gaga fixed on as a potential creative partner, but although she emailed him, she heard nothing back.

Undeterred, she pressed on with recording the album. Of course, the album wasn't just full of club bangers. Gaga wanted it to be a showcase for an idea – the idea of possessing inner fame and how anyone could feel famous. 'But it's a sharable fame,' she explains. 'I want to invite you all to the party. I want people to feel a part of this lifestyle.'

Her New York Italian roots were also a great source of inspiration for the album. 'It's who I am,' she explained. 'It's culture, it's family, it's my heritage, it's my fashion sense.

'I'm inspired by the street, but I'm also obsessed with the gangster mob princess in *Scarface* – that's not Italian, but you know what I mean – the casinos, the gaudiness, it really plays into the concept of my album, *The Fame*, because for me, Italians and that sort of gaudy culture is a way of self-proclaiming your own fame without eight million dollars.'

Her decision to make *The Fame* a pop record rather than an out and out dance record was also a deliberate choice. It stemmed from her days dancing onstage with Lady Starlight, when they decided to subvert the underground idea of 'cool' by playing pop, a genre that had become decidedly uncool. For Lady Gaga, pop was the new underground.

'Everybody said goodbye to pop for a little bit, and we really started bowing down to these rising indie acts, but I don't feel that there's anything wrong with the major label music machine,' she says. 'I remember standing outside of *TRL* with *NSYNC and Britney written all over my face and crying if I could see her hand – you know what I mean? You can't buy that – it is so intense to be a superfan.'

Gaga would get asked all the time how she managed to stay edgy and underground, but she didn't consider herself to be underground at all, other than coming from the underground. What she wanted was to reinvent the pop machine.

She remembered the Mickey Mouse Club explosion that happened in New York around 1999 and 2000, when she was in her mid teens – Britney, *NSYNC, Backstreet Boys and Christina Aguilera. She remembered how if any of those artists were in New York, the streets around Times Square were shut down and rammed full of fans.

'Since then we've lost the desire to eat the artist, and it's something I want to bring back, but in a cool way,' she explained to the *San Francisco Bay Times*.

Her days of gogo dancing with Lady Starlight and partying five nights a week in New York were also the inspiration for the dance-floor tracks on the album. Although she was in Los Angeles, which was famous for its celebrity parties and lifestyle, ironically it wasn't that kind of fame that Gaga was writing about. It was New York's underground scene, with its arty misfits, drop-outs and seedy bars she was inspired by.

'I guess you could call them seedy because they smell like urine and there's a lot of drink and drugs,' she said to The Grind. 'But they were like home. I was gogo dancing and making music, and the album is really influenced by my lifestyle. I write about things I know about – money, pornography, sex.'

But as she had decided to make a pop record, Gaga also wanted some songs that came from a more innocent place. Martin Kierszenbaum worked with Gaga on the sweet, ska-pop influenced 'Eh Eh (Nothing Else I Can Say)' (as well as on tracks 'I Like It Rough', and 'The Fame'). 'Eh Eh' was Gaga's simple pop song about finding someone new and breaking up with the old boyfriend, while 'Brown Eyes', which she wrote with Rob Fusari, was the most vulnerable song on the album.

Generally, however, the theme that ran through the album was sex, sex and more sex, a topic that American audiences and the media can sometimes have difficulty with.

'We Americans are quite hard on women for strong sexuality,' she explained to Australian magazine, *The Age*. 'But it's really who I am and what I feel comfortable with. If anything, I'm probably the only pop singer on the planet whose record label would prefer it if she toned it down. You'll never hear me say, "Give it to me, baby." I say it in a different way.'

She did exactly that with the track 'LoveGame', singing, *'I wanna take a ride on your disco stick.'*

'It's another of my very thoughtful metaphors for a cock!' she told *The Age*. 'I was at a nightclub, and I had quite a sexual crush on somebody, and I said to them, "I wanna ride on your disco stick." The next day, I was in the studio and I wrote the song in about four minutes.'

In Gaga's opinion, all music is inspired by sex, so why not make it a running theme on her album? 'It's the primal rush and instinct and the insatiable need for orgasm and procreation. Isn't that why we're all here? Love and sex are the only reason to make art.'

Deciding what tracks to put on the record and which to leave off took Gaga some time, but she certainly had a unique way of deciding. 'Writing a record is like dating a few men at once,' she said later.

'You take them to the same restaurants to see if they measure up and at some point you decide who you like best. When you make music or write or create, it's really your job to have mind-blowing, irresponsible, condom-less sex with whatever idea it is you're writing about at the time.'

In total, Gaga had spent two and a half years working on *The Fame*. During that time she had grown and matured in many ways – in her songwriting, in her performances, in her style and also as a person. In *The Fame* she had created a magnum opus – a début that would throw the pop rulebook out of the window and demand that everyone get up and dance around in glittery underwear.

The album contained songs written in a number of different styles, encompassing a number of genres. It didn't obey any conventions and, like Gaga herself, it celebrated diversity, containing some electronic dance floor bangers, a seven-minute rock opera and some sunshine ska. It was a modern musical masterpiece that perfected the art of pop and would eventually burst into popular music consciousness demanding that everyone sit up and take note.

She couldn't have been happier with the way the album turned out. *The Fame* was a reflection of her transition from her well-to-do uptown New York life with her parents, to the edgy downtown neighbourhoods of the East Village and Lower East Side. The album was all about everything she had learned on her life journey – all her experiences with boys, money, sex, drugs, drink, fashion, parties and fun.

'It's heavily influenced by fashion and lifestyle,' she says. 'It's absolutely 100 per cent a concoction of my love of 1970s glamour, 1980s synth sounds, dance club fever, disco, a lot of my melodies have a real 1950s Beatles quality, glamour, filth, rock'n'roll … I think about everything when I'm writing, but I'm constantly being influenced by different things, I'm like a little sponge.'

But her brazen, open manner of talking about taboo subjects like sex and drugs didn't go down well with everyone, as she was soon to find out. She might have made herself a hit record, but persuading the prudish American media was going to prove a lot tougher than she thought.

Chapter Eleven
Convincing the Public

Although you might have thought that making great music was the hard part, you would be wrong. Though she had made some killer records, Lady Gaga was about to find out that breaking through the barriers that American radio stations and TV shows put up would be almost impossible.

The mainstream media was having a hard time understanding what she was all about. She didn't look like anyone else around at the time. She may have been petite and platinum blonde, but she wore huge fake eyelashes that were so heavy she could barely open her eyes. And she was rarely seen wearing anything at all on her legs – Gaga hardly ever strayed from her no-trouser policy, even in the freezing New York winter.

'I've always loved rock and pop and theatre,' she explained to the world on her website. 'When I discovered Queen and David Bowie is when it really came together for me and I realised I could do all three.' She also cited Peggy Bundy and Donatella Versace as her fashion icons.

'I look at those artists as icons in art,' she continued. 'It's not just about the music, it's about the performance, the attitude, the look – it's everything. And that is where I live as an artist and that is what I want to accomplish.'

Having set out her stall to the world, there was only one thing left: to get the world to listen.

It wasn't going to be easy, but this was the tough chick from New York who never took no for an answer, and who would never accept failure as an option. Gaga was no stranger to hard work and would do whatever was necessary to get the word out. She would work her butt off, hustle and grind.

She decided that she wanted to make three short art films – which she called *crevettes* (which means shrimps in French) – which she would show throughout her onstage performances. She created the character of Candy Warhol – a female version of her hero Andy Warhol – and created a three part film called *Who Shot Candy Warhol*. The first part was entitled *Pop Ate My Heart*, the second was called *Pop Ate My Brain* and the third called *Pop Ate My Face*.

'Shrimps are small, but decadent and tasty, which is how I think my films should be,' Gaga told the *Guardian* about *Who Shot Candy Warhol*. Ever insistent that she have creative control over everything where possible, she decided to produce her *crevettes* herself, wanting them to have a sophistication and darkness that contrasted with her energetic, upbeat stage show.

Gaga's record labels decided to schedule 'Just Dance' as her first single release in North America on 8 April, but there was still a lot of work to be done. As busy as she was, believe it or not, Gaga still found time to write songs for other artists.

With Akon, she had worked on a number of songs for the Pussycat Dolls' upcoming album, as well as songs for lead Doll Nicole's solo album.

In fact, she was so involved with the project that when the Pussycat Dolls management heard Gaga's own material and saw her perform live, they knew she'd be the perfect opening act for the 2009 World Domination tour.

Even though the tour was almost a year away, Gaga jumped at the chance. She knew the Dolls had a huge fan base, and with their burlesque roots, the two acts would be a perfect match. And as she had been writing songs for them, she felt as though they were already working together. Rumour had it that the Pussycat Dolls wanted Gaga to be more than just an opening act: some sources reported that they wanted Gaga to join the group!

However, according to Showbiz Spy, she turned them down, saying she wanted to pursue a solo career: 'I was writing tracks for them at the time,' she explained, 'but I had my vibe and my own style.'

Another group that was on Gaga's radar to work with was the newly reformed New Kids on the Block, who were signed to Interscope for their new album and tour. Gaga's label approached her about the possibility of working with the boys and Gaga simply couldn't refuse.

Rather than writing a song for the New Kids, Gaga actually went into the studio to write with them. Considering they were a band she had idolised as a teenager, it was an incredible experience to be in a studio with them.

'I love them. I just love them so much, I can't really talk about it,' she later gushed to the *San Francisco Bay Times*. 'When I first met them, I almost had a heart attack. It's really humbling and incredible. Donnie took a liking to my work and writing style and loved my vibe … It's been a really incredible experience.

'I'm really a pop girl,' she continued. 'I'm not afraid of the word. I sort of strive to be, similar to the way Andy Warhol made pop art that he wanted – and it is considered today – fine art. He wanted to be taken seriously for making commercial work. That's what I want to do. I love working with pop acts. I love writing pop music. It's totally my thing. I've 100-percent conceptualised endlessly, day-after-day, new ways to make pop fresh and new and not such a dirty word.'

When writing her part on the track 'Big Girl Now', Gaga teamed up with her friend RedOne to help Donnie write the track 'Full Service' for the New Kids album *The Block*, which was scheduled for release that September.

She loved working with New Kids, especially Donnie, who she'd had a huge crush on as a teenager, and the New Kids loved Gaga too. They recognised her talent as a songwriter, and had heard her own music too, which they loved. It didn't take them long to ask her to go on tour with them at the end of the year, as one of the opening acts for their live show. They had already chosen Natasha Bedingfield and Colby O'Donis as opening acts for part of the tour, as well as Tami Chynn, who Gaga had written songs for with Akon.

The tour was a sell-out, and would be Gaga's first experience of arenas and venues that held anywhere up to 25,000 people. She was ecstatic.

Her first show with the New Kids was booked for 8 October in Los Angeles, and there were some hectic months of playing shows and promoting her own album before she would set foot on stage.

To celebrate her hard work with New Kids and a new start

in LA, Gaga decided to have a new tattoo. She'd already had a couple of tattoos done in New York when she was underage using a fake ID. She had a white daisy design on her shoulder and a peace sign on her wrist, which she'd got as a dedication to one of her favourite artists, John Lennon.

'If you look at it it's the wrong way round,' she explained in a 2009 interview. 'But when I look at it it's the right side up – for me this was inspired by John Lennon. I grew up two blocks away from the Imagine memorial, one block away from where John Lennon was assassinated, and I'm a huge Beatles/John Lennon fan, so give peace a chance.'

The reason she got the peace symbol tattoo was as a reminder to her that even though she wrote fun music about sequins, panties, fame and money, she should always keeps in mind the important things in life too.

For her new tattoo, Gaga trusted only one chick in Los Angeles to do it: the legendary Kat Von D. She'd been a big fan of Kat's work for a long time, especially her portraits and the kinky pin-up girls she was famous for doing. Kat, who had been tattooing since she was only fourteen, had found fame on the TV show *Miami Ink*, and when filming finished and she returned home to Los Angeles, she was offered a spin-off show about her own tattoo parlour: *LA Ink*.

Kat took Gaga out into the back to do her tattoo, and in the LA sun she drew a feminine design of roses and vines with some music notes, and placed it on Gaga's lower back and left side. While tattooing her, Kat asked about the history of her other tattoos.

'When I got my first tattoo, [my family] nearly had a fricking heart attack,' Gaga laughed. 'When I got the next one I felt bad because I wasn't going to tell them I was going to do it, we're really close. I went home and started crying. I was like, "I love it." My mom was like, "What's wrong with you, getting tattooed?"'

Gaga couldn't have been happier with her tattoo. It was elegant and classy and had turned out just the way she wanted it to. With her new body art in place, Gaga, the Haus of Gaga and all her label bosses began preparing to promote her records, starting with first single, 'Just Dance'.

Gaga, who incorporated visual elements into all the songs she wrote, had an idea of what she wanted the 'Just Dance' video to look like. Ever the perfectionist and control freak, she wanted complete creative control over the video, but though Interscope supported her, considering she hadn't sold any records, they weren't ready to hand over control just yet.

Instead, they hired director Melina Matsoukas, a graduate of NYU who had directed music videos for industry heavyweights like Beyoncé ('Green Light'), Snoop Dogg ('Sensual Seduction') and Kylie Minogue ('In My Arms'). Luckily for Gaga, Melina was sympathetic to her vision and created a stylized, fun video that Gaga loved and which was, for the most part, exactly what she'd envisaged.

True to her DIY roots, Gaga made the disco bra she wears in the video herself. The video also features cameos from her dancers Dina and Pepper, who enter the party with her at the start; Space Cowboy is on the turntables, rocking a mirror-ball tie and sparkly gloves; a white-suited Akon is sitting on the couch, and Colby O'Donis was on set to film his verse.

Gaga really wanted the video to be a party – a party that everyone in the world would feel they needed to be at. She also wanted to blend together the two worlds she came from: the world of educated, beautifully manicured young women, and the less wholesome world of downtown, Lower East Side kids, living for the music and the moment.

'I put the two worlds together in this video,' Gaga said on *Behind the scenes – "Just Dance"*. 'I'm about to just break down in tears, because I'm so excited and so overwhelmed, it's really incredible. The video is a visual to the last twenty-two years of my life. All of these ideas and all these things I've cared about forever are now in the room, and we're shooting it, putting lipstick on it!'

Gaga was over the moon about the video shoot. Finally, after being so broke for so long and only being able to do things on a minimal budget, she had the record label's money behind her. 'It was so fun, it was amazing,' she gushed to About.com. 'It was like being on a Martin Scorsese set. I've been so low budget for so long, and to have this incredibly amazing video was really very humbling.'

Even though the concept for the video – a house party in Brooklyn – was all about fun and partying, it wasn't all fun on set. For Gaga, this was just the first step in her pursuit of world domination – there was no time for running around partying. For her, it had to be perfect.

So everything – and everyone – was handpicked for the video: the clothes, the spaghetti, the ice-blocks, the strategically sized disco balls, the kiddie pool, the blow-up whale, the partygoers – right down to Gaga's fishnet-covered nails – her 'fishnetnails' as she called them.

'I might even seem to be a bit of a diva,' she says about how she acts on video shoots. 'I'm sort of with myself, in my work head space, worrying about costumes and if extras look right, and placement. I don't just show up for things, you know. That video was a vision of mine. It was Melina the director who wanted to do something, to have a performance-art aspect that was so pop but it was still commercial, but that felt like lifestyle. It was all those things, I love it.'

They still found time to have some laughs on set, though. The whole point about being at the party was that it was meant to be very theatrical and over the top, but Gaga's performance with the orca (the inflatable killer whale in the paddling pool) had people in stitches on set.

'Throughout the entire day, the director Melina, if you could have recorded what she was saying to me while I was performing,' Gaga laughed afterwards while speaking to an Australian radio station. 'She was like, "No, Gaga ... Stop humping the whale, Gaga ... Get up off the floor ..." But sometimes I just go into this mentally, like, crazy state!'

By the time it came to editing the video down, Gaga managed to persuade the record label to let her sit in with Melina while she worked. 'I've watched it upwards of 500 times ... Director Melina, she is a genius,' said Gaga of her experiences on set. 'She's from New York, and working with her was one of the greatest creative experiences I've had yet. My vision for the video was "a house party in Brooklyn", but with all the sentiment glamour and filth of a downtown soirée or trashfest, with a touch of my Italian gaud and fascination with mobster movie motifs.

'Having Melina as a director, I felt as if she had been with me (perhaps in my purse) for the last four years, following me during the NYC music grind. Her intuitions and attention to detail were scary,' said Gaga of the video's director.

In preparation for the release of 'Just Dance' as a single, Gaga decided to play a high-profile show to get a buzz started about her. For the stage routine, she worked with world-renowned choreographer Laurie-Ann Gibson, who's worked with artists like Brandy and Michael Jackson, as well as choreographing movies.

Gaga had met Laurie-Ann while she was still in New York. In an interview with Neon Limelight, Laurie-Ann remembers the pair of them were toughing it out to put things together when Gaga was starting out.

'We were in the Lower East Side doing nothing, getting stuff for costumes ourselves … she trusted me so much and trusted my gift. A lot of the time with Puffy and Danity Kane and a lot of other artists, they're fearful of what the music industry will think or what the record label will say. With Gaga she didn't care. I was like, "You gotta do this! You gotta try this!" And it was just the trust that really produced great work and she's such a great songwriter.'

So having put together some sassy moves with Laurie-Ann, Gaga, Space Cowboy and dancers Dina and Pepper flew to Miami to perform at the Winter Music Conference.

Chapter Twelve
Trying to Break America

To get the wheels in motion, Gaga flew out to Miami to play at the Winter Music Conference, an annual dance music event held in Miami. A hard-partying weekend of clubs, DJs, drink and other party favours, this was one place Gaga could feel right at home.

With dancers Dina and Pepper, she performed in bright sunshine on the rooftop terrace of the Raleigh hotel on a day sponsored by Armani Exchange. Wearing black ankle boots, nude tights and a leotard with a chain belt loose around her waist, Gaga strutted around the roof with her hair – now bleached a true platinum blonde – flicked around her shoulders.

The small crowd – mostly journalists – didn't know what to make of her at first. But the fun, poppy dance vibes of her set soon won them over. She won the hearts of more Miami fans that night when she took Dina and Pepper to perform at the Nervous Party at Score, a local gay bar.

The small but energetic club was packed to the rafters with gay clubbers. Gaga wore her black ankle boots, hot pants and a necktie covered in tiny mirrored tiles, as well as a silver bra, while Dina and Pepper wore black knee-high boots and leotards. Gaga's energetic performance blew the crowd away. 'She was totally nuts!' said one party-goer in the crowd.

As the show was on 27 March – the night before her twenty-second birthday – she was presented with a birthday cake shaped like a mirror ball with 22 candles stuck in. She blew the candles out and spent the night partying to celebrate her day's success in Miami.

The week after her Miami triumph, 'Just Dance' was scheduled for release in the US, but Gaga, her managers Troy Carter, Leah Landon and Akon were all finding it difficult to promote the record. Most American radio stations didn't want to play it because of the song's lyrical content, but Gaga thought it was more than that – it was also because of the musical innovation in 'Just Dance'.

'They would say, "This is too racy, too dance-oriented, too underground. It's not marketable",' she said to the *Independent* about trying to get the song played on the radio. 'And I would say, "My name is Lady Gaga, I've been on the music scene for years, and I'm telling you, this is what's next".'

She would turn out to be right, of course, but not without a fight.

'I mean, it just doesn't sound like Katy Perry's "I Kissed A Girl",' she continued to the *Guardian*. 'It's a beautiful, lovely, amazing hit record and it sounds like a radio hit. My song doesn't sound like a radio hit … In the UK it might, because electro-pop is not this stinky underground thing, it's a real genre, but in America electro-pop is dirty underground music.'

'Just Dance' was released on 8 April 2008 in America, but it didn't chart. There was only one way Gaga could think to get her musical message to her fans: to play as many shows as she could and build up a fan base that way.

Gaga became more and more excited about the creative opportunities that lay ahead of her and fantasized about topping the charts. 'I obsess endlessly about more projects for me to sink my new yawk teeth into,' she wrote on her blog. 'Writing for other artists, designing new clothes/Lady Gaga props, watching Bowie and Devo DVDs to get ideas for my show.'

As well as all this, she was still writing songs. Gaga and Space Cowboy were a fantastic creative partnership. They worked together to create all the remixes for Gaga's live shows, and were even collaborating on new songs, in particular a raunchy festive record they would put out for fans at Christmas 2008 called 'Christmas Tree'.

As well as planning for her future, throughout the month of May Gaga played an energetic show in an intimate venue almost every night, usually in gay clubs, backed up by Dina and Pepper. She was determined that if she couldn't get noticed on the radio, she would get noticed in the clubs. She played in Los Angeles, Hollywood; played six shows back in her home town New York; toured to Florida, then did four shows in San Francisco.

She had a blast being back in New York. Her tour was a mini-promo through the gay club scene, hitting the Pink Elephant, Tenjune and Mansion clubs. When she played the Campus show at Splash, she was annoyed about having to perform; she'd rather have been partying there with her friends.

'I wanted to be on E, sweating my pants off in the crowd,' she later said to *HX* magazine. 'When I play at gay clubs, it's like playing for my friends: they get it and understand what I'm trying to say, and they have a very open mind about art, pop and commercial music.'

Her touring entourage was the enigmatically named Haus of Gaga, in reference to the German art school that combined fine art and crafts into its designs: Bauhaus. Haus of Gaga was starting to grow. As well as Space Cowboy and Dina and Pepper, enigmatic art director Dada – real name, Matthew Williams – was on hand to art direct Gaga, and act as a sounding board for the creative ideas for her live show and clothes.

Dada was an ex-boyfriend of Gaga's, but she preferred him to be one of her chief collaborators than a sexual partner. 'Dada is quite brilliant and we were crazy lovers, but I stopped it when we discovered what a strong creative connection we had,' she told *The Sunday Times*. 'I didn't want it just to be about careless love.'

The Haus was also modelled on Andy Warhol's original Factory, his New York studio between 1962 to 1968, although he called all his subsequent studios The Factory too. Although the building had been destroyed, the idea of The Factory was a source of great inspiration to Gaga.

It was a hangout for artistic types, drop-outs, free-thinkers, drag queens, musicians, drug users and Warhol's collaborators, as well as being famous for its groundbreaking parties. It was this free creative spirit that Gaga wanted to recreate with her Haus.

Gaga had always felt close to alternative communities, particularly the gay scene, and her love for them was reflected by her choice of first widely broadcast TV appearance, which was for the NewNowNext Awards on 7 June 2008. The awards show was hosted on the American cable channel Logo, which is aimed at lesbian, gay, bisexual and transgender viewers.

As well as supporting the LGBT community at the awards, Gaga met one of her all-time heroes, Cyndi Lauper. Standing backstage, Gaga saw Cyndi walking past. To her surprise, Cyndi came right up to her and looked her up and down.

'You look great, kid,' Cyndi told her. 'Take no prisoners!'

Gaga could barely breathe. She had sung along to 'Girls Just Wanna Have Fun' as a young girl, and Cyndi's fashion style had always been a source of inspiration to her. She couldn't believe one of her childhood idols was actually talking to her.

Inspired by the chance meeting, Gaga went out onstage and performed her heart out, singing 'Just Dance' as the closing act of the show with great success.

The show also brought Gaga together with another great talent who would help her create some fabulous outfits. *Project Runway* star Christian Siriano was hanging around backstage and the two hit it off immediately. He loved her trashy, musical theatre style and nicknamed her 'Tranny Gaga'. She promised to keep in touch with him as she had a lot of ideas about clothes she wanted him to help her make.

Later in June, she gave one of her first big interviews to About.com, which asked her about her use of the word 'retrosexual'. Gaga replied, 'I'm so obsessed with all things retro, the 1970s and 1980s. I don't know, that word just kind of flew out of my mouth one day, and it stuck with me. I often do that – if I coin terms, they'll become like the centrefold of my entire project or an entire record'.

About.com also asked her how she was bridging the gap

between dance music and hip hop, since she was signed to Akon's Kon Live, which is an urban label. 'I actually wouldn't consider myself a dance artist,' she replied. 'I think I'm bridging the gap in a few different ways, and it's mostly from a music conceptual standpoint, mixing the dance beats one second. Mixing retro dance beats with more urban melodies, and a certainly pop chorus. It's really about, in a very methodic way, almost choosing exactly what pieces of what I want to have in the record, and then watching it cross over, with my fingers crossed.'

At the end of June 2008, the first of a weekly series of video diaries (called *Transmission Gagavision*) was broadcast on her website. The first of these was an introduction to Lady Gaga, and featured her in a cab in San Francisco talking to Space Cowboy. It also showed Gaga's first appearance in *Entertainment Weekly*, appearing on a gossip page where she had been noted for her outlandish dress (a leotard and round sunglasses).

Also present in the *Transmission Gagavision* videos was dancer Dina, but notably absent was Gaga's longstanding back-up dancer, Pepper. The Gaga entourage had been in San Francisco to play shows for the city's annual Gay Pride celebrations and Lady Gaga was reported to have said that because Pepper had refused to play one of the Pride shows she had been fired.

The gay community were very important to Gaga. She recognised that her songs and performance were pretty camp, and she had had nothing but good experiences playing at gay clubs.

'I had a lot of gay friends, growing up, I went to a lot of gay clubs,' she told MTV. 'Dance in the gay community is this subculture of celebration of joy and fun. I draw lots of my inspiration from the gay community, in an almost subconscious way it's so deeply ingrained in me now. It's so joyful.

'Sometimes I say, as long as it's gay, just make sure it's gay – like for the video, or for the mix on something, or for the clothing, I say as long as it's gay, it's good.'

In fact, Gaga was so supportive of the gay community that she was chosen as the closing act for San Francisco's 2008 Gay Pride show on 29 June 2008. Before going onstage, she sat in a booth near the main stage, signing autographs for the hundreds of fans who were gathered there to see her in the blazing sunshine. Dressed in a white latex jumpsuit – a conservative look compared with her usual uniform of leotard and fishnets – Gaga took time during her performance to speak to the crowd. 'Thank you, California, for legalising gay marriage,' she said. 'It's about time!

'I never really decided to be this kind of artist,' said Gaga to GayWired.com about her close relationship with the gay community. 'It's just who I became and I think it was just a result of my lifestyle … you know … just hanging out with people who are gay, transgendered or cross-dressing males and females.

'You're a product of your environment and, without even realising it, the music and the show began to speak to that community. And they've been so open and welcoming and I love them back.'

Gaga always looked forward to playing her gay club shows because she found the audiences so welcoming. 'I think that's because they know [my show] came out of that community and was inspired by that community. It's very much a part of who I am … The theatre, the drama, the drag show, just became a love of mine.'

When the *San Francisco Bay Times* asked why she thought her show appealed so much to lesbian, gay, bisexual and transgender audiences, Gaga had to think for a moment. 'They get it a little more,' she answered. 'Sometimes in straight clubs, the girls give you the "Who the hell are you in your panties?" look. It's like the minute I'm in these clubs, for whatever reason, the gay community sees the concepts. They see the references. I can see them pointing out, "Oh, that's the Madonna shoulder pad!" Or "That's the this or that." I just love it.'

Gaga's sights were set on making her live performances bigger and better. For the moment her performance was based on her and her dancers with Coco, a long-time ally, replacing Pepper, and her only prop was her disco stick. It was handed to her when she was onstage, and used to light up when she danced with it. Now Gaga wanted more gadgets and more technology; it was almost all she could think about.

She found it hilarious when journalists, intrigued by her onstage prop, would ask her to tell them about her disco stick. All she could think of was the countless other gadgets and props she was going to bring to her live performances in the future. For the moment, however, restricted again by a lack of funds, she just had to hustle these performances, try to get her songs played on the radio and try to sell records. Then all the money she made could be spent on her live show.

She was asked to perform live at a show for Perez Hilton, the notorious celebrity blogger, who was throwing an Independence Day party in Las Vegas. The show, held at legendary night spot Privé, won her throngs of new fans from the audience and behind the scenes. Perez Hilton loved her energetic performance and camp stage show and befriended her then and there. He – and his blog – would loyally support Gaga from here on, determined to get her the coverage and publicity he felt she deserved.

One piece of publicity that got her noticed around the world was via a high-profile TV appearance. She appeared on the 57th Miss Universe Pageant on 14 July 2008, which was held in Vietnam and hosted by Jerry Springer and Spice Girl Mel B, who introduced Gaga as a worldwide superstar.

Flanked by her two dancers, who were dressed in black with bright yellow shoes, Gaga wore a black latex catsuit and her trademark killer heels. She gave a mind-blowing performance of 'Just Dance', making all the pristine beauty queens in their swimming costumes look positively plain and boring in comparison. If the crowd didn't know who she was before, they certainly did afterwards.

The next day, the number of fans on Gaga's MySpace page shot up by hundreds. She had definitely made an impression, and with the show being aired in hundreds of countries across the world, she had managed to reach an international audience.

This audience included German fashion designer Michael Michalsky, who had heard about the New Yorker on the Internet, and was a massive fan of her track 'Paparazzi'. He invited her to his show, the Michalsky Fashion Show at Uferhallen Mercedes-Benz Fashion Week in Berlin. Recognising her immense talent and sense of style, the designer invited her to walk the red carpet before the show, and sit in the front row – the greatest honour that can be bestowed on anyone invited to a fashion show.

Wearing a strapped yellow ribbon dress, a red jacket with pointy shoulder pads and a loose hood, Gaga was relatively unknown in Europe at the time, leading one blogger to say that 'she just looks like a random run-of-the-mill red carpet crasher, only I don't see any exposed nipple.'

But it was here at the show that Gaga was to have one of her most bizarre encounters with the paparazzi. When she stepped out of the limo, there was a rush of around thirty photographers from fashion magazines around the world, clamouring to take pictures of her, asking, 'Bella, bella, who are you?'

She told them her name was Lady Gaga. They started screaming her name and asking her to turn round and pose for them.

They don't even know who I am, Gaga thought to herself. They think they should know who I am, but they don't. 'If she's famous and I don't know about her, then it becomes, "Oh yeah, I saw Lady Gaga,"' she said later in an interview with Blogcritics. 'I'm really not shy about how slick it is,' she added. 'It's very slick, but to me. It's an art form. If Andy Warhol did it, I can do it too.'

Her ideas about fame – and what she wanted to achieve from the release of her album – were becoming clearer too.

In another *Transmission Gagavision* video, dancer Dina said to Gaga, 'I feel like you're a force to be reckoned with, and anybody who comes in contact with you can't help but be under your spell. Like you're a puppeteer. It's an influence. I feel like I'm working with an artist who's moulding me. What do you want *The Fame* to do?'

'I want it to do that!' replied Gaga. 'I want people to find a sense of inner confidence and fame for themselves that has nothing to do with being famous. We're not famous, but we feel "the fame".'

Regardless of whatever inner fame she felt, Gaga was

starting to get noticed more by the American public. And an interview she would give to gay magazine, *HX*, would ensure that this fame was about to hit another level.

Chapter Thirteen
CONTROVERSY

In the August issue of gay magazine *HX*, Gaga made an admission that would come back to haunt her.

'Are you really as boy crazy as your lyrics suggest?' the magazine asked.

'Yeah. Well, I'm girl crazy, too,' replied Gaga. 'It really depends on where I am. I love men, I love women and I love sex, but I'm actually pretty introverted right now because I'm so enveloped in my work, and it's hard to let anybody near that. People f*** with your energy, and it's very hard to find people that are supportive of your art and don't want to take time away from it. A lot of times, boyfriends and girlfriends get jealous and want all your attention, and I really don't have time for that.'

HX went on to ask the burning question, 'Do you consider yourself bisexual?'

'Sure,' said Gaga. 'I mean, I don't really consider sexual orientation in general. It's like, people are born the way they are.'

In her typical, brash way Gaga had spoken openly about drug taking earlier in the interview, and now she had told them she was bisexual, too. Although coming out of the closet is more accepted in mainstream American culture than it ever has been before, there's still a hardcore conservative population who think it's immoral.

More than that, the media jumped on Gaga's throwaway comments about her sexuality as an attempt to piggyback on the hype surrounding another artist who had broken onto the scene earlier that year: Katy Perry. Her controversial track 'I Kissed A Girl' had been released in May, going on to become a global smash, reaching number one in twenty countries worldwide, but it had drawn criticism from the media, both gay and straight alike. Gossip singer Beth Ditto told *Attitude* magazine that she thought the song was 'a boner dyke' anthem for 'straight girls who like to turn guys on by making out or like faking gay'.

'I hate Katy Perry!' said Ditto. 'She's offensive to gay culture, I'm so offended. She's just riding on the backs of our culture, without having to pay any of the dues and not being actually lesbian or anything at all. She's on the cover of a f***ing gay magazine.'

Although Gaga wouldn't be drawn to say anything negative about Katy Perry, who she had met, and liked, she was upset that the media thought she had only made her comments to get a slice of Katy's publicity and almost stopped talking about it altogether in interviews. 'It's actually something I don't really like to talk about any more,' she said when interviewed by *Fab* Magazine. 'I'm kind of disappointed by it all. I don't like to be seen as somebody who is using the gay community to look edgy. I'm a free sexual woman and I like what I like. I don't want people to write that about me because I feel like it looks like I'm saying it because I'm trying to be edgy or underground.'

But the interview also served to win Gaga support from some quarters, including her new friend Perez Hilton, who posted a link to it on his blog saying, 'Welcome to the gayborhood!' Perez – and others, who knew Gaga's history and long-standing admiration for the gay community – knew that her comments weren't about publicity at all.

August was a month of upsets and controversy. At a performance in New York for radio station Party 105 on 9 August, Gaga accidentally smacked dancer Dina in the mouth with her microphone while onstage. Within seconds, there was blood streaming from Dina's mouth and she had to run offstage to a waiting ambulance.

Poor Dina lost three teeth and had to have them capped by a dentist. She soldiered on to appear in Gaga's next performance at the MTV Studios in New York, though for one of the last recorded episodes of *Total Request Live*, the show that Gaga had turned up to as a teenager, screaming for Britney Spears.

Also attending the show were the Jonas Brothers and the rapper TI. Wearing a red hood over her red leotard, lacy white tights, heels and black shades, Gaga looked every inch the superstar, although her individual sense of style set tongues wagging after the show.

Working hard to promote *The Fame*, which had been scheduled for release in the United States on 28 October 2008, Gaga worked the red carpet, talking to as many presenters and journalists as she could. She had no problem getting their attention:

with her red leotard and 'no trousers' rule, she was perfect news material.

Undeterred, she carried on with her crazy schedule, just as she had been before. Melina Matsoukas had done such a good job on the 'Just Dance' video – with Gaga feeling she was sympathetic to her vision – that Interscope called her in to work with the Haus of Gaga again on the 'Beautiful, Dirty, Rich' video.

In the end, they released two versions of the video: the official one and another one cut with clips from the TV show *Dirty Sexy Money*, which was created to promote the series.

The video featured Gaga and an entourage in a mansion, frolicking with bundles of cash. There were shots of Gaga screwing up notes and lighting rolled-up notes like cigars. Her dancers Dina and Coco also featured in the video, as did Space Cowboy.

Dirty Sexy Money wasn't the only show that used Gaga's music to promote it. 'Paparazzi' featured on *Gossip Girl* – a show Gaga loves, describing it as 'very entertaining' – and *The Hills*. In fact, Gaga was getting used to hearing her songs in the background when she watched TV. 'It happens all the time,' she told *iProng* magazine.

'I call the record label and I'm like, "Oh my god, I didn't know that song was on that show." There have been so many licenses recently that I don't even hear about all of them,' she went on.

'But that makes me feel great because it tells me that my goal, which was to analyse and reckon and struggle with ideas about pop culture, it's really working because all of these shows that are so emblematic of modern television and modern film and modern movies and modern club shows, it's like they're all gravitating towards my stuff, because I guess it's speaking to something that's very today.'

It's no wonder Gaga was used to hearing her records in places she didn't know about; her label had managed to get twenty-five TV and film placements of her songs before *The Fame* was even released.

Jody Gerson, who signed Gaga's publishing deal with Sony/ATV, said it wasn't difficult to get the tracks placed. 'The networks and supervisors just loved her.' By the summer of 2009, songs from *The Fame* would have been placed in TV shows or films over 100 times (the most requested song being 'Just Dance', followed by 'Poker Face' and then 'The Fame').

The radio stations might still be resistant to playing her records, but Gaga was getting across to her public through TV shows. 'Just Dance' was also finally starting to make it in the charts, partially due to Gaga's killer live performances.

The track was a club hit in America, peaking at number two on both the Hot Dance Airplay and Hot Dance Club Play charts. But they were still having trouble getting mainstream success, and she and the label felt they weren't getting the full support of the American media.

There was no time for tears, though. Gaga's hectic schedule meant there was another promo single out soon – 'Beautiful, Dirty, Rich' – closely followed by the album's second proper single, 'Poker Face'.

Unwilling to let Gaga take complete creative control for the video again, the record label brought in Norwegian video director Ray Kay to direct the video for 'Poker Face'. Ray Kay was behind the helm for videos like the Backstreet Boys' 'Inconsolable', Beyoncé's 'Freakum Dress' and Christina Milian's 'Say I'.

Young Hollywood visited with Gaga on the set of the video and filmed the interview as Gaga was getting made up ready to perform. Perhaps mindful of the tender age of the audience of *Young Hollywood*, Gaga censored her usual explanation of the song – that it was about being with her boyfriend, but fantasising about being with a woman at the same time – or perhaps she was still wary of being accused of stealing Katy Perry's 'bisexual' limelight. Whatever the reason, she gave her interviewer another interpretation of the song.

'The song is about the way that girls catch guys,' she said, 'and how you got to keep your poker face, because the minute you let him know how much you like him, he runs for the hills.'

For the video, Gaga dressed in a couple of striking outfits, her favourite being the black, all-in-one scuba latex outfit that, in Gaga tradition, she made herself.

The video featured her with her dancers and Space Cowboy, playing strip poker round a table. When the other girls lost they took their clothes off, but Gaga's bra has a lock on the side, so it has to be unlocked before she can remove it. This chastity-style bra was another Gaga invention, made by the Haus of Gaga especially for the video.

For those who look closely you can see a lot of poker in the details of the video, including Gaga's fabulous eyelashes with diamond shapes on them, which she got from the exclusive Tokyo Lash Bar in London, and her fantastic poker-chip false nails.

Gaga was delighted with how the video turned out. As with all her videos, she had had a vision, and Norwegian director Ray Kay had helped her realise it. She had sent a sketch of what she wanted the blue outfit, which she wears while dancing by the pool, to look like, and the result was an electrifying blue outfit with cutaway sides.

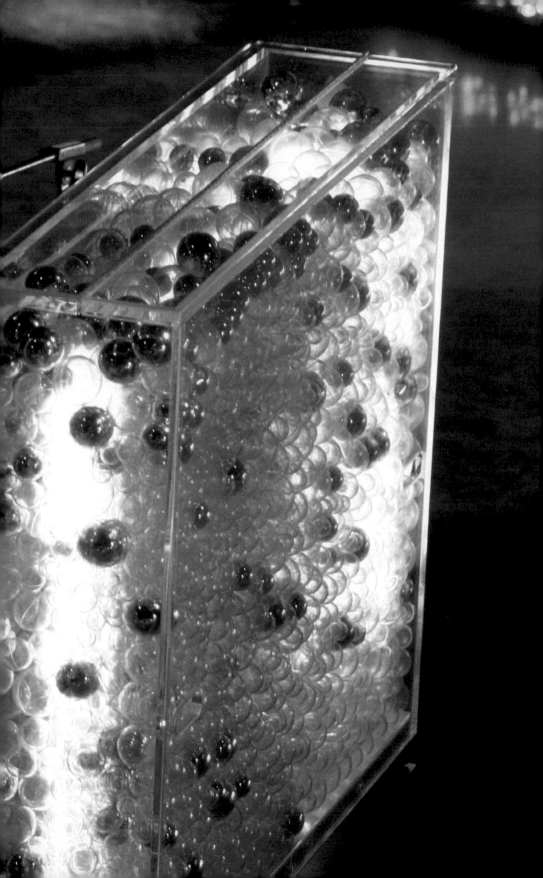

You might think Gaga's many costume changes and eye for detail would have been the biggest problem of the shoot, but in fact it was the two Great Danes who appear in the video. According to *MTV News*, no matter how many times they attempted to shoot the opening scene where Gaga emerges from the pool, the dogs would not co-operate.

'Those dogs just wouldn't sit still, and they wouldn't do what we wanted them to do,' said Kay. 'There were two dog trainers on each side of the shot, trying to hold the dogs down in the position they were supposed to be in, but they just kept getting up or looking in the wrong direction … So, actually, we never got the shot in-camera the way it's shown in the video. We had to combine different takes of the dogs to get the shot the way it is in the video.'

The release schedule for *The Fame* was staggered across different countries, due to come out first in Canada in August 2008, then Australia in September, then the United States and Italy in October, Germany in December, and finally the UK in early 2009.

With all the tracks written, mixed and mastered, the album was finally coming together. But when it came time for Gaga to choose the track listing, it took a while to whittle down the best cuts. In the end, she decided on twelve tracks running in this order for the standard version, which was released in Canada, Australia, and in some European countries: 'Just Dance', 'LoveGame', 'Paparazzi', 'Beautiful, Dirty, Rich', 'Eh, Eh (Nothing Else I Can Say)', 'Poker Face', 'The Fame', 'Money Honey', 'Again Again', 'Boys Boys Boys', 'Brown Eyes', 'Summerboy', 'I Like It Rough'.

It also took Gaga some time to choose who to say thank you to in the album's liner notes. There were many people she had to thank – all the people who had helped her dream become a reality. In particular she wanted to thank Vincent Herbert, chairman of Streamline Records, who she felt had really recognised her potential as an artist.

Gaga also included a poem for her aunt Joanne, her father's artist sister who had died at only nineteen. 'I always felt a very strong connection to her,' Gaga told Wild 94.9 in San Francisco. 'For whatever reason, I believe that I have two hearts, and in some way my life and this music is meant to finish up the rest of life that she did not get to live. So for me, my motivation is to fulfil the destiny of Joanne.'

Having sorted out the track listing and liner notes for the album, and with the 'Poker Face' video cut and nearly ready to be sent out, Gaga could get back to concentrating on chart domination – which wasn't happening for her in America.

She shouldn't have worried, though. In other countries around the world fans were going totally gaga for her, in particular in Canada, where 'Just Dance' had topped the charts and the newly released album *The Fame* was at number one in the digital download charts. When she found out, Gaga couldn't believe it and broke down in floods of tears.

Gaga, dancers Dina and Coco and Space Cowboy spinning records and rapping in the background all took to the stage at the Dragonfly Nightclub in Canada's Niagara Falls, ecstatic about the record's success there. It was truly a night for celebration, and an opportunity for Gaga to send a lot of love to her Canadian fan base.

Gaga's touring schedule was gruelling, but at a gig in Las Vegas she got to hook up and perform onstage with her friend Akon. In the blistering heat of Las Vegas, Gaga performed to throngs of sweaty fans at club Rehab, promoting *The Fame*. Even though in typical Gaga style she was only wearing a black leotard, hood, red gloves and fishnets, it was still incredibly hot.

As she was coming to the end of her set, she beckoned to Akon, who was standing at the side of the stage. She whispered in his ear as Dina and Coco continued to dance to the backing track that Space Cowboy was laying down. Akon put his arm around Gaga, lifted her up and, to the delight of everyone there, threw her into the crowd!

She crowd surfed over her fans, loving the fact that she got to be in the audience for part of her show. Akon stood on stage laughing, clapping and cheering for her.

Many music blogs later featured pictures of Gaga crowd surfing, and most mentioned that this wasn't the first time Akon had thrown someone into the audience. At one of his shows in 2007, Akon was performing onstage when someone in the crowd allegedly threw something at him. He asked the crowd to point out the guilty party. One of his security guards picked a fifteen-year-old boy out of the crowd and sent him to the stage, where Akon picked the kid up and threw him into the crowd. The boy landed on another kid in the audience who suffered concussion, and the whole incident ended up with Akon being taken to court. He pleaded guilty, but instead of having to go to prison, he was sentenced to 65 hours community service and a $350 fine.

Luckily, though, there was no such tragedy in Las Vegas, just a crowd full of sweaty Gaga fans getting an eyeful of their pop icon as she surfed right over their heads!

Thinking that Gaga looked like she was having a good time, Akon decided to crowd surf as well. The audience went wild, spraying bottles of water up in the air in an attempt to cool off from the summer heat.

Shortly after the gig, Akon and Gaga were interviewed together. Knowing that his presence would draw more attention to Gaga and her music, Akon went with her to countless radio stations and shows, trying to spread the word of Gaga. He knew that she only needed a little push from him before people would realise how talented she was.

When visiting *B96*'s morning show, the presenters asked Akon what advice he had given his protégé. He thought for a second. 'None,' he said, then after a pause he joked, 'Stay off drugs.' Everyone in the studio laughed.

'Seriously though,' Akon continued. 'None. But she's so smart already. She gets it. She's been around so long, she's seasoned. It's almost like picking her up after all her training, all the experiences, all the hard grinding, and now she's ready. She sells it.'

Akon's faith in Gaga was well placed. Her gigs were getting better and better and he knew the hit records wouldn't be far behind. Gaga was beginning to be recognised as a star – and not just in the US.

Chapter Fourteen
Hectic Schedules

Elsewhere in the world, fans were starting to fall in love with the chick from New York in a big way, not least in Sweden, where she was invited to headline the NRJ music festival held in Stockholm on 30 August.

An audience of 50,000 people greeted Gaga when she went onstage and she couldn't believe they were all there to see her! She wasn't opening a show for anyone or playing a support or promo slot. To see all those thousands of people singing along to her songs almost made her cry.

September 2008 was a truly international month for the singer. Accompanied by dancers Dina and Coco, as well as Space Cowboy, she got to visit Holland, where she played the Valtifest festival in Amsterdam on 6 September. The festival had a dress code that asked partygoers to come dressed in fluorescent colours which, to Gaga, looked amazing.

The next day, back on the other side of the world, hundreds of music industry starlets and heavyweights were getting ready for one of the major events of the year: The MTV Video Music Awards, held at Paramount Studios in Hollywood. On the tour bus, the Gaga entourage crowded around Space Cowboy's laptop, which was plastered in Gaga lightning bolt stickers, to watch the show. They got quite a shock when they saw Christina Aguilera take to the stage to sing 'Genie In A Bottle' and 'Keeps gettin' Better' for the audience. Dressed in a black latex catsuit, with a black eye mask, metal wristbands and long blonde hair, at first glance she bore an uncanny resemblance to Gaga.

The music blogs went ballistic after the show, with angry fans accusing Christina of ripping off Gaga's style of dress and song – 'Keeps gettin' Better', with its more electronic, edgy production, sounded uncannily like 'Just Dance' – whilst also accusing Christina of lip-syncing and missing her dance steps.

Angry Xtina fans retaliated on their own blogs and on the forums on Christina's website, stating that it was Gaga who was copying Xtina's style.

Ever the diplomat, Gaga didn't want to make any enemies and certainly didn't need to engage in any kind of press warfare to get herself noticed. She had always done her own thing when it came to fashion and style, and besides, she had been a fan of Christina's ever since she first released 'Genie In A Bottle' in 1999. She had a lot of respect for the former Mickey Mouse Club star, and for all artists.

Keen to play down what was being said on the blogs, Gaga spoke out in an interview with *Blender* magazine. 'A lot of people have been saying that she is copying my style with her new song. I guess it bears somewhat of a resemblance, but I wouldn't say she is copying me. This type of dance music is becoming more popular and I don't blame her for wanting to make and perform it. Her performance was great and ['Keeps Gettin' Better'] is a hot track.'

Hoping she had managed to smooth over the spat before it started, Gaga and her entourage moved on with their international schedule, heading to the UK, where she was due to play two shows in London. The first was at gay night OMO at the London Astoria, where stars like Patrick Wolf and Craig Template were spotted in the audience, bopping away to Gaga's beats. A few days later, she also played *SuperSuper* magazine London Fashion Week Party at London's elite Punk club, in Soho.

Gaga loved London. Space Cowboy took the chance to point out some of the city's underground gems to her, and she made sure she had time to check out the crazy street fashions in Camden and Portobello Road, picking up inspiration wherever she went, hoping to use what she saw for the headline tour she and her managers were planning for 2009.

As well as Amsterdam and the UK, Gaga also found time to play two shows in Paris and Marseille, France. Determined to pick up some style inspiration, she popped into some museums while she was visiting in Europe, where she came across a dress she had seen before on the runways in 2007. It had blown her away then, and seeing it now, the feeling was just as intense.

The dress she had seen was Hussein Chalayan's infamous bubble dress, with hundreds of inflatable plastic spheres strung around a set of bandages. She snapped a picture of it on her phone and sent it to Dada, who was back in LA, saying how beautiful it was in real life. She wondered if they could make something like it for her to wear in the future.

Although she loved nothing better that spending quiet hours wandering around museums, she didn't have much time for it. Soon Gaga and her entourage were hopping on a plane to Australia for the last shows of her mini tour, before heading back to Los Angeles to start touring with New Kids on the Block.

It was a rough flight to Australia. The flight was twenty-six hours anyway, and as if that weren't bad enough, there was a problem with one of their planes. It had been a fairly uneventful flight until the captain lit up the 'fasten seatbelts' sign, at which point Gaga knew something was up. 'Ladies and gentlemen, please return to your seats,' said the announcement. 'There's no need to panic, but there's something wrong with the engine. We will be on the ground in five minutes. Please fasten your seatbelts.'

Gaga fastened her seatbelt and gripped onto the hand rests. 'It was the longest f***ing five minutes of my life,' she said later. 'The rate of descent was super fast. It's so crazy. I didn't cry until we hit the ground. I held it in, I was talking to Jesus, then we hit the ground and I lost it.'

The flight had given her quite a scare. She played a packed gig in Sydney, and arranged to do a lot of publicity while she was there, but it felt like the shaky start to her trip was a bad omen.

She had arranged to play live on Australia's Channel 7 *Sunrise* programme, but the morning of the show Gaga was really ill. She turned up to perform, but her voice was pretty shaky, so she agreed with the sound engineers to mix her voice into the backing track, as she still wanted to perform live. The show's presenter, Mel Doyle, appeared embarrassed when it looked like Gaga was lip syncing to the backing track, and the performance led to the singer being slammed on several music blogs, and was picked up by the local press.

Even a killer gig in Melbourne the following night – where the line to see her stretched 50 metres down the street outside the Inflation nightclub – couldn't cheer Gaga up after what had happened on the show.

In retaliation, she wrote a blog on the *Sunrise* website. 'I was sick the day of the show but I absolutely, 100 per cent, was singing live. I have never lip-synched and never will. Even on my worst day, I never will.'

'I was so sick that day,' she recalled later when asked about the incident by a Danish journalist. 'I had been doing two shows a night for a month and a half. I lost my voice, and I did sing, but we mixed it in with the track very low. I didn't think it was very nice, the station for no reason made these incredible claims about it.

'If you were just a regular person you could have listened to it and heard that I was singing. I don't need to lip sync, I can sing. I do do music that is very heavily electronicised, and I like to have the track in there. I like it to sound like the record. To be perfectly honest, what other people think about my creative decisions doesn't mean so much to me.'

If anything, the one thing Gaga didn't want was to be underestimated as a performer, or written about as merely a pop songwriter, knowing that she was a great performer who could write songs too. She was the real deal, and she didn't want to be written off as a wannabe or someone who hadn't earned their musical stripes.

She made sure to stress in every interview that she wrote all her music herself and that she was actively involved in all the creative content of her videos, short films and TV appearances. 'I just really care about what I do,' she summed up to About.com.

But the fact remained that her music was very electronic. In live shows, many performers who couldn't sing well would use live auto-tuning to correct bad notes – the bad part of that, of course, was that the person singing sounded digitally enhanced. Paris Hilton made use of the technology for an entire album.

Despite the fact that Gaga had vocal chords to challenge Mariah Carey's in a warbling competition, most of the tracks on her album had been auto-tuned purposefully to give them that electronic sound, particularly 'Just Dance' and 'Poker Face'. So perhaps she should have expected the media to think she couldn't sing.

'It's not for my voice,' Gaga explained to the *Telegraph*. 'The radio is used to a certain perfection and it compresses the voice in a certain kind of way. It smooshes all of the sound together so it sounds smaller but fatter; it's not open, very condensed.

'Unless you are Duffy, where it's this extremely organic record, it's important to play into the psychology of the listener, who is used to a certain sonic quality in the voice. If they don't hear that, it's not hip,' she added.

Gaga shouldn't have worried though. Her fans – who had queued around the block in Melbourne and Sydney to see her live – knew she could sing and were awestruck by her performance. This was reflected in her record sales there: her album débuted in the Australian chart at number 12, and 'Just Dance' had just hit number one! The single was also number one on the iTunes chart, three on the ringtone download and number one on the Weekend Top 20 countdown.

Chatting on the phone to members of the Haus of Gaga back in New York, she prepared to come back to the United States and start touring with the New Kids. There was good news from America too. 'Beautiful, Dirty, Rich' and 'Poker Face' had both been released as e-singles and were creeping up the Billboard chart, though neither were the immediate chart smashes she knew they were capable of being.

She hoped that the tour with New Kids on the Block would cheer her up, but in reality she had no idea what she was about to experience.

Chapter Fifteen
Touring with New Kids on the Block

Arriving back in LA from her disappointing trip to Australia, Gaga consulted with the Haus of Gaga immediately. She knew she was going to have to up her game and prove herself to the crowds – and the media – while performing on the New Kids tour.

When setting up the tour, New Kids had given Gaga and her management the budget for her opening performance.

'I went through it, then I submitted what I wanted, all the technology, all the things I wanted to build, all the fashion that I wanted to put in the show, and it was wildly over budget,' Gaga had told a journalist in Australia.

'They said, "Gaga, how are you gonna pay for this?" So then me and my manager showed them my touring schedule, where every night after each New Kids show I'm going to play another full set at a club in the city that's going to pay for all the overage from the tour, and I'm not gonna pocket a dime.'

Although this seemed like a crazy concept to the journalist – as most pop stars were usually in it for the money – Gaga tried to explain herself. 'For me, it means nothing to make the money if the show is not a complete freaking orgasm for me onstage, because I live for it, that's it.'

Working with the Haus of Gaga, who included choreographer Laurie-Ann Gibson, she decided to change the performance onstage. The pair worked together to choreograph an insane live performance that would get remembered – and unfortunately, that meant changing the dance line-up from two girls – Dina and Coco – to four hunky guys, who she would dance with and who could lift Gaga up, adding another dimension to the dance.

She also brought three giant LCD screens onstage, and collaborated with her friends at the Haus of Gaga to create some new costumes for her. She was determined to make her live show something the arena crowds would remember.

The New Kids had already started their tour by the time Gaga joined it. They had held the first two dates at the Air Canada Centre in Toronto, Canada. The opening show, like all the others on the tour, had been a sell-out, and the boys had British pop sensation Natasha Bedingfield opening for them.

Gaga joined New Kids, Natasha and the rest of the touring posse in Los Angeles on 8 October. Even though she was opening the show, which meant going onstage early at 8p.m., she knew it was a chance to win hundreds, perhaps thousands, of new fans.

Beforehand, she took the chance to have a quick look round the huge venue. The tour had been so successful with the few dates the boys had already played that the merchandise stalls were running low on New Kids goodies, like key chains, lockets, lanyards and badges.

Gaga couldn't believe it. She remembered wearing her 'I love Donnie' T-shirt with such pride as a kid, and here she was, about to open the show for one of her favourite childhood bands.

As an opening act, her 30-minute warm up set was far too short, but she gave it her all with her dancers and Space Cowboy there to support her. The arena was far from full – as it was so early there were only around 7,000 people there – but she was determined that when they left they'd remember her.

She opened her set with 'Beautiful, Dirty, Rich,' and came out from behind the LCD screens, which were showing a video of her in her sunglasses wearing bright orange lipstick. Throughout the set she showed off new choreographed dance moves that included her being lifted up by her dancers and riding one of them like a horse, all the time managing to sing live while jumping up and down, pumping an arm in the air.

She got out her famed disco stick for the set closer, 'Just Dance', then bounced offstage to an arena of cheers and screams.

Although she was happy with her performance, she wanted to watch other professionals from the wings, so she ran back to the stage to watch Natasha Bedingfield woo the crowd with songs like 'Piece of Your Heart', 'These Words (I Love You, I Love You)' and 'Put Your Arms Around Me', finishing her set with her best-known track, 'Unwritten', which is also the soundtrack to the TV series *The Hills*.

Then it was time for the New Kids. Before they came on, the giant screen at the back of the stage lit up with a question:

'Are you ready?' And an arena full of screeching women screamed back their reply, 'YES!'

Gaga couldn't believe it. It was completely insane. The women were going crazy – some were crying; some were shouting, 'Oh my God! Oh my God!' repeatedly; some were leaping up and down. Hundreds of tiny little screens – either cell phones or cameras – were pointed at the stage.

The New Kids gave an incredible performance. Gaga forgot she was there as a performer and joined the screaming crowds, jumping up and down and clapping for Joey McIntyre, Donnie Wahlberg, Danny Wood and brothers Jordan and Jonathan Knight.

Although she had had a Donnie T-shirt in her youth, Gaga didn't want to pick a favourite out of the boys now. 'I love them all. They are the nicest guys on the planet. They are so cool and so talented and so motivated. It's been fifteen years and they fricking hit that stage like it's 1986!' she laughed. 'If you brought a camera with you, all you'd see is flying bras and screaming girls.'

The New Kids played some of their greatest hits, such as 'You Got It (The Right Stuff)', 'Please Don't Go Girl', and 'Baby, I Believe in You'. They also played seven songs that Gaga had written for them from their latest album.

It was an incredible night and Gaga couldn't believe how lucky she was to be on tour with such a huge group – and such nice guys too.

'I learned the ropes from them,' she said later of her time on tour with the New Kids. 'They treated me with such an incredible amount of kindness. It just taught me that a kind heart goes a very long way, even in this business.'

As well as opening for the New Kids, Gaga continued to

play shows under her own name, trying to win over as many new fans as she could and take her place at the top of the charts.

She travelled back to San Francisco to do a mini tour around some gay clubs, and she was astounded at the audience that turned up to watch her. They were such a diverse crowd – there were straight teenagers, drag queens and hip-hop cats. She tried to find a common theme in her fans, but just couldn't.

One thing Gaga had become aware of was that her music seemed to unite many different kinds of people. In an interview for *BlackBook* magazine, a journalist picked up on this, and on the fact that her appeal was cross-racial, since she worked with R&B artists like Akon.

'Yeah, it's really true,' Gaga agreed. 'It conquers race boundaries in terms of the audience, and I also cross sexual boundaries, with straight audiences and gay audiences. It's funny, I just played a show in San Francisco, and it was supposed to be a gay night at a club, and it was not just gays. It was gays, it was straights, you know, men and women. It was black, it was white, it was Asian – it was everybody all showing up on a gay night.'

It wasn't just the gay clubs of the United States that were taking Gaga to heart either. Across the world, people were starting to sit up and take note. And in addition to the recent controversy over Christina Aguilera's performance at the VMAs, another celebrity impersonation was about to take place.

Across the Atlantic in London, ex-Spice Girl Mel B, who had introduced Gaga to the world while presenting the Miss Universe pageant earlier that year, turned up to the MOBO awards in a distinctly Gaga-style dress. It was tight, gold and knee-length, which wasn't in itself remarkable, but the loose hood and up-twisted hairstyle had Gaga written all over it. Newspapers and fashion commentators across the world noticed it, as did Gaga's friend Perez Hilton, who pointed it out on his blog.

Celebrity blogger Perez Hilton had been won over by Gaga's sweet nature, her empathy with the gay underground movement and her energetic performances. He was so enamoured with her he became an instant Gaga supporter, and in return Gaga had given Perez Hilton's website the world web premiere of her video for 'Poker Face', which had drawn thousands of hits and hundreds of comments when it was posted. So when Perez was planning a show in New York on 24 October, he knew there was no one he'd rather ask to headline than the wonderfully innovative New York chick herself.

Gaga was beside herself with excitement. Perez Hilton had booked out The Highline Ballroom for the event, One Night In New York City, part of the 2008 CMJ Music Marathon & Film Festival. Situated on 16th Street, The Highline Ballroom is a legendary New York nightspot that Gaga had visited for gigs and club nights as a teenager. But tonight she was headlining!

Beforehand, Perez interviewed the acts and managed to catch Gaga for a chat before she went onstage. Once again, however, Gaga's big mouth was about to cause her trouble.

When he asked what had inspired her album, she replied cheekily, 'Cocaine!' After Perez told her he didn't promote drug use, she brushed it off and said, 'A Thierry Mugler dress from the 1980s. What inspires me? Andy Warhol. I love Madonna, David Bowie, Sinead O'Connor, I mean, I could go on and on forever!'

They changed the subject quickly, and Gaga started telling Perez why she thought it was about time pop music made a comeback. 'I'm particularly arrogant about pop music, and think that it's amazing,' she said. 'There's nothing more powerful than a song you can play anywhere around the world, at any time, no matter what, and everybody gets up and dances.'

For One Night in New York City, the warm-up acts were beginning to take to the stage. These included Sharon Jones and the Dap-Kings, and Yo Majesty and Semi Precious Weapons. SPW were longstanding fixtures of New York's live music scene, as well as being friends of Lady Gaga and Lady Starlight from their gogo-dancing days.

Lead singer Justin Tranter strutted around the stage calling the audience 'bitches', while the crowd screamed for their tongue-in-cheek hard rock. In between each set the drag queens in the crowd had dance-offs with each other, grinding, flirting and pulling each other's fake boobs and hair.

With her trusty troupe of male dancers, each with black make-up painted around their eyes like masks, Gaga sashayed onto the stage. Gaga had a dedicated hardcore fan club everywhere she went, but particularly in her home town. Fans fought with each other to get to the front of the audience, screaming so loud it was almost impossible to hear anything onstage. Meanwhile Gaga strutted her stuff onstage and the audience lapped it up.

The show went down in history as one of the most raucous and colourful she'd ever played. The music blogs buzzed with stories of her victorious performance, though there were always haters, trying to do down the Lady's success.

Brooklynvegan's review of the show had a list of comments after it, where people remembered Gaga from her days on the

Lower East Side: 'Does anyone remember when lady Gaga was a girl named Stefanie who used to play piano and do singer-songwriter stuff at The Bitter End...' posted someone who called themselves 'Mike'.

A reader calling themselves 'Brussel Sprout' responded, 'MIKE: I do remember that ... She used to hang out at St. Jerome on Rivington all the time ... I can't count the number of times I've done blow with her in the bathroom ... She's really not cool at all.'

Another reader, who preferred to remain anonymous, weighed in to the discussion with, 'She is gross, used to see her all the time too down at jeromes with her skeevey 80s hair metal bartender boyfriend (luke?)'

There were always going to be haters, and Gaga wasn't going to dwell on them. In her opinion, there would always be people who didn't understand her or what she was trying to achieve – and there was no point wasting her time on them.

All in all, the Perez show was a victory. But there was no time for celebrating, as the New Kids tour continued to roll on. The first few shows that Lady Gaga had opened for them weren't full to capacity, and as they toured through Sacramento, San Jose and Las Vegas, the arenas remained half full when Gaga hit the stage.

But for the Madison Square Garden Arena show on 27 October – back in her home town of New York – it was another matter. It was a happy coincidence that on the same day as Gaga got to play a show in her home town, *The Fame* was released in the US. And it wasn't just any show, either – Madison Square Garden is one of the biggest venues in the city.

That day, there was a record release party in the Virgin Megastore in Union Square. Hundreds of fans turned up and queued around the block, desperate to catch Gaga perform in-store. Inside it was total chaos. Gaga had her full stage layout with her, including four dancers and three huge LCD screens. Every show she played was the same, whether she was rocking a huge stadium or playing an intimate gig for a hundred fans.

Gaga ripped through her set, and was so excited to be there she did her old trick of crowd surfing – not once, but twice! She climbed up on the railings at the side of the stage and jumped into the crowd, managing to surf back onto the stage within ten seconds, mercifully without injuring any of her fans with her killer heels.

Back on the tour bus, there was barely time to shower, brush her extensions out and suck down a protein shake before heading to Madison Square Garden to open the show for the New Kids.

She was so excited to be playing one of the biggest venues in New York. It had been her dream ever since she was a child, and here she was, about to go onstage!

'I have played every club in this city thinking it was the Garden!' a breathless Gaga told the crowd onstage. 'Remember that tonight, a star was born!'

After showing off her tight choreography to the screaming crowd, Gaga finished 'LoveGame' and ripped off her frilly skirt to sing 'Paparazzi'.

She ended the energetic set with 'Just Dance', then ran off-stage a little choked up. She had just performed onstage at one of the biggest venues in New York. Her family and a bunch of her Lower East Side friends had come to watch the performance and were amazed at how well their beloved Gaga was doing.

Despite giving it her all onstage, backstage there were

nerves in the Gaga camp. *The Fame* had just been released in America. The record had already gone to number one in Canada and it had stayed in the top 15 since its release in Australia, but it was proving tough to break America. The radio stations and media were wary of Gaga's unconventional brashness – the way she didn't care about what anyone thought and the fact that she just wanted to make music and art.

In the end *The Fame* entered the US chart at a very respectable number 17, and was number five in the iTunes top albums chart.

The reviews, however, were mixed. *Slant Magazine* gave the album three and a half stars, and some damning praise, 'Gaga's lyrics alternate between cheap drivel ("I wanna take a ride on your disco stick") and nonsensical drivel ("Drive it, clean it Lysol, bleed it/Spend the last dough in your pocko!"), and her vocal performances are uneven at best, successfully tossing out dirties on "Beautiful, Dirty, Rich" and painfully enunciating without any semblance of sex appeal on "LoveGame".'

Entertainment Weekly were kinder, but still only gave the album a B score. '"The Fame" is remarkably (and exhaustingly) pure in its vision of a world in which nothing trumps being "beautiful, dirty, and rich".' In this economy, though, her high-times escapism has its charms.

Even though 'Just Dance' had gone to number one in Canada and Australia, and *The Fame* was riding high in the charts of both countries, chart success in America continued to elude Gaga. So, determined to work as hard as she physically could after what she thought was a disappointing chart performance, Gaga cranked her schedule up a notch, cramming in as many shows as she physically could in the time available.

After the Madison Square show the night before, Gaga had played another two performances and hadn't slept by the time the New Kids tour moved to Atlanta. Still Gaga opened for the New Kids at the Arena at Gwinnett Center, but somehow had the energy for a midnight show at Atlanta club Bazzaar.

The club was full to capacity – perhaps over capacity – and everywhere there were screaming fans, many of whom had taken the care to dress up like Gaga. Everywhere she looked there were handmade disco sticks and lightning bolts on people's faces.

'I f***ing love Atlanta!' said Gaga when interviewed by a journalist there. 'I'm in heaven. I've got fans here!'

Even though playing so many shows was exhausting, Gaga was on autopilot. Her only goal was to promote the record until it went to number one.

'It has just been so fun. I don't even care that I haven't slept,' she said. 'I just want to kill for his record. I'll stay up four, eight, ten days if necessary. We played Madison Square Garden last night. I've played every club in that city, and to actually play the Garden was a dream.'

Ever appreciative of the fans who supported her, especially the ones who had turned up dressed in Gaga-wear, she made sure she let the journalist know that her fans meant everything to her. 'I just want [the fans] to know that I love them, and thank you so much for supporting me. The record is really about inner fame and that you can take that fame and make it if you want to.'

Gaga was giving everything to music. She had given up on partying – she was on the road 24/7 and had cut out of her life any thoughts of a boyfriend or lover. Instead she spent her time trying to persuade the press that Lady Gaga wasn't a stage name or persona; it was who she really was. On 28 October, the day *The Fame* was released, she gave an interview to the *New York Post*, trying to dispel those rumours.

'We're just not used to artists having really strong sensibilities about fashion, art and visuals and everything tying in together, so people assume that "Lady Gaga" is a character, and it's totally not,' she explained. 'I've always been somebody that stands out in a crowd. I've been making clothes for myself and dressing the way I do for a really long time, so it's not a look for me, it's my lifestyle.

'The way that Andy Warhol attempted to make commercial art that was taken seriously as fine art is the way I want to make pop music – pop art performance and pop fashion that's taken seriously as high fashion and highbrow,' she went on to explain to the journalist, alluding to the work of one of her all-time heroes.

Making it was something that was clearly on Gaga's mind. But chart success was going to have to wait, because first, the controversy over Christina Aguilera's style was going to hit a whole new level.

Chapter Sixteen
Controversy With Xtina

Although Gaga thought she had put out any potential fires with Christina Aguilera over the star's choice of outfit for the MTV Video Music Awards, she couldn't have been more wrong. On 11 November, Christina was interviewed by the *Los Angeles Times*, and the journalist asked her what she thought of the people who'd been saying she was stealing the Lady's style.

'You know, that's funny that you mention that,' Christina replied. 'This person [Lady Gaga] was just brought to my attention not too long ago. I'm not quite sure who this person is to be honest. I don't know if it is a man or a woman. I just wasn't sure. I really don't spend any time on the Internet, so I guess I live a little under a rock in that respect.'

Later on in the day, music and fashion website TMZ weighed into the controversy, posting a picture of Gaga in her white crystal origami dress, with long platinum blonde hair and bangs next to a picture of fashion designer Donatella Versace with the caption, 'What was that about Xtina copying someone's style?! We're just sayin'.'

Music blogs and forums went wild in support, with irate fans allying themselves with 'Team Gaga'. Some theorised that Christina had paid TMZ to put the comment on there just to put Gaga down.

Furthermore, some fans, who had been loyal followers of both Gaga and Christina, couldn't believe Christina was capable of being so mean. On Lady Gaga's website forum, one fan wrote, 'I've always been a Christina fan my entire life ... until now. TEAM GAGA!'

Music lovers traded blows in comments posted under news stories about the feud, declaring themselves Team Xtina and dismissing Gaga as some jumped-up, wannabe imposter. The accusations were wild and unrestrained, with one fan writing, 'She's a f***ing nobody – everyone will have forgotten her in six months.'

Dismayed by what Christina had said about his friend, Gaga's pal Perez Hilton flew into action to rescue the situation. He posted two pictures on his blog – one of Gaga from the 'Just Dance' video shoot six months before, where she's wearing her loose, white leopard print top. He then posted a new publicity photo of Christina that had just been taken with a black and white striped top and strong eye make-up that looked very similar to Gaga's look.

Still on the road with New Kids and travelling through Omaha and Denver, the Gaga camp stayed quiet and didn't respond to Christina's comments. Gaga had too much respect for Christina as an artist, and besides, she had spent months and months working on her costumes with the Haus of Gaga.

Her influences were more classic 1980s fashion and 1970s pop art rather than any look a contemporary of hers was rocking. She had always been inspired by fashion. 'I'm inspired by fashion in such an intense way,' she had said earlier that year on *Making The Fame*. 'When I write music I think about the clothes that I'll have on when I'm singing it. I really dress for the part and make music for the dress.'

Besides any kind of immediate similarity, Gaga just couldn't believe that Christina Aguilera – a Grammy-nominated artist who had been releasing hit records for ten years – would actually know who she was! In her mind, she was still a small fish in a big pond, working her butt off for recognition. The idea that artists who were her idols might know who she was – that was outrageous!

In another interview with MTV just two days later, Christina laughed off suggestions that she was copying Gaga's style, insisting that she was influenced by artists like Sia and Goldfrapp.

'I was very inspired by the look and feel of that [pop-art] genre, your Jane Birkins, your Blondies, females who have come before who have done this so many times and so well – almost as a homage to them,' Christina said.

'Also, speaking of Warhol, Nico from the Velvet Underground ... so it all kind of ties in to a pop-art feel and twist, with a mod look. But a futuristic taste of what's to come.'

For the hardcore Team Gaga, this was adding insult to injury. They knew that Gaga had been saying openly that Andy Warhol was a major inspiration to her. The interview she gave to the *New York Post* earlier that year had quoted her as saying, 'I want to make pop music, pop art performance and pop fashion that's taken seriously as high fashion and highbrow.'

Team Gaga – who counted celeb blogger Perez Hilton amongst their ranks – were up in arms.

'Listen, it's OK to get inspired by other musicians,' said Perez. 'But don't lie about it, Aguilera!!!!!!'

Gaga carried on travelling around with the New Kids for their tour. But as more blogs and music press picked up on the story of the alleged friction between Christina Aguilera and this new, super-talented artist Gaga was attracting more and more fans.

The publicity – along with the word of mouth about her awesome stage show and performance – led to those huge arenas getting full earlier and earlier with people wanting to see Gaga's show.

Her live show – with four backing dancers throwing themselves around the stage, carrying her around, then laying on their backs holding her keyboard on their feet – was something Gaga was really proud of. She had worked hard to make her show memorable and different, and people were starting to recognise and appreciate it as just that.

'The show is just me doing what I feel comfortable doing onstage,' she explained to Blogcritics. 'It's just like my raw energy. Before I knew it, I was known as an exhibitionist, theatrical performer. That's just kind of what happened. I never really tried to do that. If anything, I tried not to do that and gave up on trying to stop being myself.'

For Gaga, it made no difference whether her audience was five people or 50,000 people, she always made every performance her best. 'You have to work very hard; nothing is handed to you,' she continued to Blogcritics, when they asked her what advice she had for young, up-and-coming artists trying to make it in the music business.

'If you can't handle it in downtown New York, you can't handle it out in the world. If you're interested in making a life in art, you better be ready for the struggle – there's a lot of it.'

Even though Gaga wasn't nominated for an American Music Award, her record label Interscope hosted an after party for the show. The televised award ceremony had a huge list of celebrities attending, including Rihanna, Beyoncé, Mariah Carey, Miley Cyrus, Alicia Keys, the Jonas Brothers, New Kids on the Block, and an artist she had a lot of admiration for: Kanye West.

The after party was an exclusive, invite-only selection of celebrities, industry insiders and general hangers-on. In front of an audience that included names like Will.i.am, Enrique Iglesias, T-Pain and Jordin Sparks. As well as the Haus of Gaga and her managers, Gaga's friend Colby O'Donis was there to support her for the show.

Gaga put on an incredible thirty-five-minute show that got everyone on their feet and dancing, inspiring whoops and cheers when she announced to the crowd that *The Fame* had just gone gold. Even though the event was only for celebrities and bigwigs, a couple of dedicated Gaga fans managed to win tickets and gleefully posted photos of the show on Gaga's forums, gushing over how awesome the performance was and how lovely the Lady was when they'd met her in person.

By the time the New Kids tour had reached the show at the Cox Arena in San Diego on 25 November, word had spread and the arena was completely full by 8p.m. when Gaga came on stage. She was over the moon. Thousands of people were there to see what all the media fuss was about, but Gaga didn't care. If they were there, it meant she could show them what she was made of.

While she was in San Diego, as well as playing the show, Gaga was interviewed for Earsucker, who took the opportunity to ask her about the comments that Christina Aguilera had made about her.

'Christina Aguilera said that she didn't know who you were or whether or not you're a man or a woman. Any comment on that? I thought it was rude,' said the interviewer.

'I don't take offence to it,' replied Lady Gaga with all the class of a real lady. 'I'm inspired by androgyny and David Bowie and Grace Jones.'

And even though the interviewer went on to ask Gaga about Christina's MTV performance and whether she thought the ex-Mickey Mouse Club star had stolen her look, Gaga wouldn't be drawn into a tabloid fight. She had seen too much bitching and fighting in the tabloids and she knew that wasn't the kind of artist she wanted to be.

'The performance bared a resemblance,' she replied to the interviewer, but continued in her usual, dignified manner: 'I don't have a look. I dress like this all the time. I have no enemies.'

Gaga's fans were delighted, Perez Hilton in particular, who said, 'That's how you properly handle situations like that! Take note, Xtina.'

Gaga's fans loved her because she wouldn't be drawn into bad-mouthing any other artists. They loved her because she was bringing something new to pop music, and she brought it with style, and good manners. She wasn't bitchy, and she never promoted herself by putting other people down. She was a real class act, and she set herself apart from the other artists who tried to win points over each other in the tabloids.

The media storm was good publicity for Christina too,

which was great for her, as she had just released a new Greatest Hits album. But through the whole affair, it seemed to be Gaga who came out on top: winning herself thousands of new fans, and strengthening the bond with her existing fans. Everyone was happy to be part of something new and exciting happening in pop music – happy to be part of Team Gaga.

Likewise the publicity was spreading Gaga's name around the music press. Even the alternative music press started taking an interest in the catfight. People who had never heard of this chick from New York heard that somewhere, Christina Aguilera was bad-mouthing some up-and-coming new artist. So they started Googling Gaga and listening to songs on MySpace.

Never put off by negative publicity, Gaga continued performing, managing to fit in a couple of shows outside of the New Kids tour. She even found time to stop off in Toronto for the day to lend support to the RE*Generation initiative, working with Canadian organisations that support at-risk and homeless youth. She also performed a benefit concert at Circa, with all the proceeds going to help shelters for homeless youths across Canada.

Before the show, Gaga – dressed in her white origami crystal dress – even took some time to look around Eva's Phoenix, a youth shelter in the city, to hang out with the kids. 'This is a really amazing, transitional place,' she said afterwards. 'If I can be inspiring to them and be a part of it, that makes me feel more powerful than any of the stage drama or the flashing lights.'

All the publicity she had got from the Christina Aquilera scandal and her charity work soon reflected in her position in the charts. In the first week of December, 'Poker Face' was number one on the digital download chart in Canada, and it had been at number one in Australia for four weeks! But still chart success in the States wasn't happening.

Fans on the forum discussed this strange phenomenon with each other, wondering why she was so much more popular outside America than inside.

Pleased by how well 'Poker Face' was doing around the world, if not necessarily back at home, Gaga headed back to her hometown of New York, where she was headlining the city's annual Z100 Jingle Ball. The Jingle Ball had a special place in Gaga's heart. Exactly ten years ago she had attended the Jingle Ball as an excited twelve-year-old music fan: it was her first experience of live music.

Everyone in the city was excited about Gaga performing there – and not just her friends and family.

'It's a great story,' said programme director Sharon Dastur. 'A New York kid opening for Jingle Ball. When we knew her song was going to be one of the biggest hits on the station, we told her people we wanted her for Jingle Ball and she burst into tears.'

And even though the Jingle Ball organisers were worried the slow economy might affect ticket sales, with Gaga on the bill, tickets sold faster than ever.

The main performance included acts like Katy Perry, Leona Lewis, Paramore, Ne-Yo and Rihanna. Along with Brandy and The Veronicas; Gaga played the opening to the pre-event show, held at New York's Roseland Ballroom.

Not only that, Gaga got one of her first tastes of what it means to be famous by getting a whole load of free stuff. Backstage there was a gift lodge, full of merchandise like digital cameras and beauty products, from the sponsors for all the artists to take.

Gaga couldn't believe it. 'I'm just a girl from New York,' she exclaimed while she was back there. 'So if there's free stuff, you know someone's going to be taking it!' Gaga was so excited about the gift lodge that she accidentally poked singer David Archuleta in the face while giving him a hug ('poke-er face, get it?' she laughed afterwards) with one of the crystals on the headpiece for her white origami outfit.

Before she went onstage, Gaga was interviewed for Z100, and she could barely contain her excitement. She had listened to Z100 radio station constantly as a kid, and she had vivid memories of the first Jingle Ball she'd attended years ago.

'Brandy, Monica, GooGoo Dolls!' she exclaimed, remembering that year's line-up. 'I was like freaking out when the GooGoo Dolls came out, and then it started snowing!'

After the pre-show event at Roseland Ballroom, Gaga and all the other artists who were performing made their way over to Madison Square Garden. Gaga's parents and sister had come to see her, and they were all hanging out backstage. Gaga was still amazed at the fact that she was attending the Jingle Ball – as a performer. It just didn't seem real at all. But things were about to get even stranger. Her mum Cynthia came over to her and said excitedly, 'Bruce Springsteen is here with his kids, they are big fans of yours!'

Gaga looked round, and sure enough, Bruce Springsteen was there with his two sons and his daughter.

She started going crazy. There was the man whose records she had listened to repeatedly with her father when she was just five years old. She knew the lyrics to his songs off by heart. She knew every chord, every progression, every key change.

Not even waiting to reply to her mum, Gaga ran over towards the seats where Bruce and his family were sitting. Too impatient to walk around the rows, despite wearing high heels and her white origami crystal dress, she climbed over the seats and gave Bruce a big hug!

'He told me I was sweet,' Gaga said afterwards. 'Then I had a massive breakdown – I cried on the man's neck!'

Despite her Jingle Ball triumph – and meeting one of her all-time heroes – nearly all the journalists who interviewed her just wanted to know more about the Christina scandal. *Fab* – a noted gay magazine – interviewed Lady Gaga and recalled what Christina had said about her, asking, 'Does she not have anything better to do than be a bitch?'

'I was not at all offended because I feel like she was just picking up on something that I'm trying to do with my work,' giggled Gaga, who wouldn't be drawn into trading blows. Besides, as she pointed out to *Fab*, 'What's so bad about being a tranny?'

'I happen to think Christina is extremely talented and I was always a big fan of hers when I was little,' she continued graciously. 'When someone calls you up and says that Christina Aguilera said something about you in the press you gotta be like "What is going on?"'

Even though *Fab* and other publications wondered whether Christina was trying to diss the transvestite look, Gaga certainly wasn't. 'I love trannies!' she said. 'Whenever I look really crazy and I'm trying to explain it to people, I tell them I'm looking like a hot tranny mess today, and that means I'm looking fabulous.'

Gaga's love of fashion was totally integral to the music she was making: the fashion, the technology and being innovative with what people would see and hear at her shows. She wanted people to leave her shows wondering what on earth they had just seen.

'In other words, it's like a pop show fit for a museum,' she said to Killahbeez. 'Everything we do is completely spur of the moment. I don't usually know what I'm wearing until it gets delivered an hour before the show and it's usually stuff you can't just get anywhere.'

But despite her best efforts, Xtinagate was a scandal that wasn't going to disappear easily.

Chapter Seventeen
Escaping Xtinagate

Despite Gaga trying to get the paps to talk about something other than Xtinagate, the subject kept coming up, again and again. Quick to defend his right-hand girl, even Akon weighed into the argument, telling *Rap-Up TV*, 'I definitely feel that Christina Aguilera is very inspired by Lady Gaga. It's almost identical. She was never doing that before Lady Gaga came out.'

Although it had been unpleasant, Gaga had managed to ride the Xtinagate storm, and it certainly hadn't done her any harm. In fact, the number of fans she had on MySpace had almost doubled during the scandal.

By handling it the way that she had – refusing to be drawn into a cat fight, or trying to score points over one of pop music's biggest global stars – she had shown all the class of a great artist. And in the meantime, she had won herself thousands more fans, who never would have heard of her if it hadn't been for Christina's comments.

Since its release in September, her album *The Fame* had remained pretty much in the Australian top ten, peaking at number four during the height of Xtinagate. In Canada, too, the album had gone to number one. Single sales had also risen, and in America *The Fame* was going up the charts again.

Over the water in the UK, avid music fans couldn't wait for the album's UK release, which was scheduled for 12 January. 'Why do we have to wait longer than everywhere else to get it?' demanded angry fans on the forums of Gaga's website. If nothing else, waiting for it longer was making them want it more.

To please her rapidly growing global network of fans, Gaga released the raunchy Christmas record that she and Space Cowboy had written together earlier in the year when they'd first started working together. Called 'Christmas Tree', it was a tongue-in-cheek, electro hip-hop Yuletide future classic.

Ever grateful to her pal Perez Hilton for his support – particularly over Xtinagate – Gaga gave the world premiere exclusive of the 'Christmas Tree' track to his celebrity blog.

She still wouldn't be drawn into saying anything negative about Christina, no matter how much the tabloids provoked her. If anything, Gaga called their bluff by praising Christina. 'She's such a huge star and if anything I should send her flowers, because a lot of people in America didn't know who I was until that whole thing happened,' she was quoted as saying in *OK!* magazine. 'It really put me on the map in a way.'

Gaga had no hard feelings about Christina's comments. In fact, she was just excited that her fans had recognised her style.

'Even though I've only been on the commercial market for seven or eight months, I've really burned graphic images of my visuals onto the irises of my fans,' she continued. 'They saw a huge, Grammy-winning star who's been around for years and they recognized Lady Gaga. That to me is quite an accomplishment.'

The visual part of Gaga's work was hugely important to her, and always has been. Her love for artists like Madonna and David Bowie was strengthened by their clever use of visuals to convey their music to people. Though some people ridiculed her outlandish dress sense, when Christina Aguilera had come out with a look similar to her own, she knew she was onto something.

'For me, I would much rather have two beautiful dresses that are like art pieces that are clear defined shapes and imagery that I hammer into everybody's brain around the world, as opposed to having fifteen pairs of jeans and jackets, where I'd always be in something different, but it's not memorable,' she explained to a Danish journalist who had asked her about her crazy dress sense.

And Gaga's look was definitely memorable. Other celebrities were picking up on this and incorporating her style into their own wardrobe in an attempt to stay on-trend.

Wannabe lookalikes were turning up everywhere, and when those lookalikes were celebrities on the red carpet, it just served to confirm what Gaga knew all along. With the Haus of Gaga, Lady Gaga had created a look and a style that was the bleeding edge of fashion.

Luckily for Gaga, she didn't have to fend off Christina questions for too much longer. On the tour bus heading to another show, her phone rang. She sighed, worried it was going to be another request for comments over Xtinagate, instead it was the record company. Streamline Records had just heard the news that 'Just Dance' had been nominated for a Grammy award for Best Dance Recording!

Even though she was up against stiff competition from Daft Punk, Hot Chip, Rihanna, and her idol, Madonna, Gaga's label felt she had a real chance of winning the award. 'Just Dance' had been hugely successful, even though it still hadn't made number one in America. Gaga felt that winning would only be the cherry on the icing. Just to be nominated alongside underground artists like Hot Chip, dance heavyweights like Daft Punk, or pop music legends like Madonna was enough of an honour for her.

Looking towards the British release of *The Fame,* Gaga started gearing up the dates of her performances at gay clubs throughout the UK, as well as opening for the Pussycat Dolls, who had invited her to tour with them in Europe in early 2009.

As 2008 drew to a close, there was still time to cram in some more Christmas shows in the US, as well as take a flying visit to Europe to play three Nokia shows in Stockholm, Copenhagen and Oslo, where the crowds went crazy for Gaga's black catsuit and her golden origami crystals.

She was interviewed in Denmark by *The Voice*, so she had the opportunity to tell her northern European fans a little more about herself.

'I'm really different from a lot of artists,' she explained. 'I'm not doing this to make a ton of money and then go to Hawaii. Every dollar I make I put back in my show.'

The Danish journalist seemed confused. 'I thought you loved money, because of "Money Honey"?'

'No,' Gaga laughed. 'Money is not on the agenda. I want

kisses first, then love, then money!'

In reality, all the money she had made from her extra shows in the autumn had gone towards paying for the LCD screens and her origami outfits. Plus she had a lot of grand plans for stage design and new costumes that she wanted to wear for the Pussycat Dolls tour, as well as on her own tour, *The Fame Ball*, which would take her around the world in 2009.

Gaga often had difficulty explaining that she wasn't particularly interested in money, especially to journalists, who were used to seeing pop stars covered in bling, living in million-dollar mansions. 'What use do I have for a Rolls Royce?' she said to one of them. 'I can't drive!'

Even though some artists would have balked at the gruelling touring and performing schedule Gaga embarked upon, she never complained once. As a girl who had been hustling for a long time in New York, she had seen a lot of talented artists go nowhere, so she knew how lucky she was to get this far.

She was interviewed with Valentine for The Grind, who asked her what advice she had for other artists who were hoping to make it in the industry. She advised them first to read her favourite book, *Letters to a Young Poet*, by Rainer Maria Rilke.

'Live your life as if you would die if you were forbidden to make music,' she added. 'If you do that, you will get your song played on the radio. It's such a difficult life doing what we do, but it's a blessing. Yeah I've got to give up a ton of things that nobody wants to give up, but every day I get to make music – it's so worth every sacrifice.'

She knew that anyone who had a dream could make it happen if they devoted their life to it. She had devoted her life to her dream, and after years of hard work it was coming true for her.

Flying back to the US on 22 December for a couple of days off before her New Year show at Webster Hall in New York, Gaga sat with Troy, her manager, and talked about the crazy journey she had been on that year. She had managed to get through several media scandals relatively unscathed, including her unintentional 'coming out' and Xtinagate. She'd also had to overcome other, more personal problems. She'd stopped updating her personal Facebook page as she was inundated with friend requests from fans, and as much as she loved her fans, she didn't want them seeing all the private photos that had been put there by her friends or family. Even her sister Natali had also started getting hundreds of friend requests from fans, desperate to get a little closer to their pop hero.

She spent Christmas 2008 with her family, who celebrated her successful year so far. Her records had finally been doing better in the US charts too, with 'Just Dance' climbing to number three in the American Billboard Christmas singles chart. She was only kept off the top by Beyoncé, whose single 'Single Ladies' débuted at number one, and Rihanna and TI, whose track 'Live Your Life' was at number two.

As she reached New Year's Eve 2008, she thought about the year that had passed and started making resolutions for 2009. Ultimately, she just wanted to keep making music – making her art. As the year had progressed, she had been spending more and more time working on her music, and not just music for her, songs written for other artists too.

She had long lists of artists and producers she wanted to work with; the creative possibilities seemed endless. And for someone as addicted to working as Gaga, that was almost more exciting than anything else.

One artist she definitely had her eye on working with was

well-known but weird goth rockstar Marilyn Manson. A surprising choice for a plastic pop princess perhaps, but they shared one thing in common: a love of shocking people.

'He is such a visionary and his work is really artistic, in the same vein as what I do,' she explained to Killahbeez. 'I would love to work with someone who has the same philosophy as I do.'

Little did she know that the freaky rock star was keeping an eye on her from a distance, and that in a matter of months the two would meet, and he would be trying to get her to date him.

Another thing Gaga hoped for in 2009 was a simple wish: just to keep healthy. At the start of 2008 she had still been partying heavily in New York. Now she wanted to save all her energy for writing music and performing onstage, so she gave up partying pretty much altogether.

She stopped drinking, apart from the odd glass of red wine, her one vice. She was working out a lot – cardio and weights so she could feel like 'superwoman' onstage. Her managers Troy and Leah made sure she ate well and kept her strength up for all the dancing she did, which meant drinking protein shakes as well as eating proper meals.

Gaga didn't mind the sacrifices. Unlike most twenty-two-year-old girls, she didn't mind giving up the chance to have boyfriends and date. 'It's not my job, it's my life,' she told *Fab* of being a musician and being addicted to the creative buzz.

'I enjoy doing this stuff. Sometimes I meet artists who are like, "Oh my god, I can't wait to go on vacation," and I'm thinking to myself: My life is on the road. I'm not on the road waiting to go home and live my life. I'm on the road living my life, having a f***ing great time, making art, staying inspired, calling the Haus of Gaga back in California and telling them,

"Hey, I saw this amazing piece in a museum and I wanna do this and I took a photo, let's do this."

'I'm so in it for the work, I just love it,' she continued. 'Next year I just wanna keep upping the ante for myself as creator, and keep getting better and better. In the next ten years I want to have a museum installation.'

For her New Year's Eve show, Gaga couldn't think of anywhere better to perform than Webster Hall. Not only is it one of the most flamboyant venues in New York City, it meant that she was home for the New Year, and all her New York friends could come and see her perform.

The show was incredible. Webster Hall had a license to sell alcohol until 8a.m., and packed in four floors of beautiful people to celebrate the New Year. Over 100,000 balloons had been blown up and tied to the ceiling in bags, waiting for midnight to ring in, when they'd be dropped from the ceiling.

The place was crazy – completely full to bursting with screaming party people. Before 'Paparazzi' she walked from one side of the stage to the other, trying to clear the beer bottles. 'There's f***ing booze all over the floor!' she joked, handing beer bottles to the security staff in the wings. Then she walked back to centre stage and smiled at the crowd, who she had to shush to get them to listen to her story.

'One year ago today, on New Year's, I was on top of a bar in a quite leathered condition, gogo dancing on the Lower East Side for money! And now I'm ringing in the new season with all you people.' She laughed before launching into a song about the only man she'd ever loved – 'Papa – razzi'.

She finished her set and, as the clock struck midnight, 100,000 balloons dropped on the crowd and Gaga made a wish: to get to number one in America. She remembered being a child, screwing up her eyes really tight, and wishing to be a pop star. She'd worked hard and she'd achieved her dream. She just knew she had to keep fighting and fighting to reach the top.

Of course, it wasn't all work. Gaga did allow herself to celebrate a bit on New Year's Eve, though her head was still full of plans. There was a lot of work to be done by the Haus to get the show ready for her tour with the Pussycat Dolls in a couple of weeks' time, but at least for a little while, Gaga could indulge in her love of red wine and dancing the night away.

Chapter Eighteen
Happy New Year

Somewhere, somebody was obviously listening to Lady Gaga's New Year wish. Even though the first week of 2009 was spent hard at work with the Haus of Gaga, rehearsing for the upcoming Pussycat Dolls tour, her single 'Just Dance' finally reached the number one spot in the US Billboard chart, some eight months after its release!

Gaga was in her small apartment in Los Angeles, getting ready to go to rehearsal and over the moon about the US chart victory when her phone rang. 'Just Dance' had just been released in Britain, and she wondered if she was being called about how it was doing.

She answered and it was her label, Streamline Records. 'You're number one in the UK!' label exec Vincent Herbert told her excitedly. '"Just Dance" is number one in the UK!' The record had knocked *X Factor* winner Alexandra Burke's version of 'Hallelujah' off the top of the charts. And as if that wasn't enough, 'Just Dance' had sold more copies than 'Hallelujah' on downloads alone.

Gaga listened to the news, stunned. She sat down on her couch and broke down in tears. She couldn't believe it. From fighting her way around at the bottom of the charts to being number one in America and Britain!

She couldn't have been happier. 'It's been a long running dream to have a big hit in the UK,' she told the *Daily Mail*. 'My fans there are so sexy and the people are so innovative and free in how they think about pop culture and music.'

There was more good news, too, as 'Poker Face' was grabbing number one single spots around the world, topping the singles charts in Sweden and Australia.

For many the chart success was a long time coming. Akon had known he had a hit on his hands when Gaga had written 'Just Dance', but they'd struggled for a year trying to persuade mainstream radio bosses to play it. 'It was a huge club record but radio wouldn't pick it up and I couldn't understand,' he said. 'I was like, "This is the biggest club record on the street!" I knew we just had to keep pushing it and in the end it was the fans picking up on it that put it where it went, not the radio execs.'

Over the moon, Gaga headed to dance rehearsals with Laurie-Ann Gibson and her dancers. But as happy as she was, she held off celebrating: Laurie-Ann was a tough dance instructor, and she knew she had to get all the steps right or she'd get a telling-off.

As well as preparing for her tour, Gaga found time to head into the office of Cherrytree Records, her label at Interscope, and perform some stripped-down versions of her songs. She performed 'Poker Face' as an acoustic song with just her on the piano, then with Space Cowboy on keyboards she played minimal versions of 'Just Dance' and 'Eh Eh'.

The performances were recorded ready to be shown on the Cherrytree Records website. But Martin Kierszenbaum, Cherrytree's chairman, thought she'd done such a great job that they would release the performances as an EP too.

After recording sessions at the Cherrytree offices, Gaga headed straight off to work on some videos. Interscope had called in the director Joseph Kahn to shoot 'Eh Eh' and 'LoveGame' with Gaga on the same weekend in early January.

Joseph had been making award-winning videos for fifteen years for artists like Britney – he made the video of 'Toxic', one of Gaga's favourite Britney singles – Janet Jackson, Backstreet Boys and the Pussycat Dolls. And even though they were shooting the videos in Los Angeles, Gaga chose a New York setting for both of them.

For the sweet, poppy love song 'Eh Eh', the inspiration had been Little Italy in New York, and the video featured the two harlequin Great Danes, Rumpus and Lava, who had been in the 'Poker Face' video. The video showed Gaga talking to her friends and walking through the streets of the city, as well as cooking dinner for a man while only dressed in her underwear.

'I wanted to show a different side of myself – perhaps a more domestic girly side,' Gaga said to PopEater. 'And I wanted to create beautiful, stunning 1950s futuristic fashion imagery that would burn holes in everyone's brains!'

The fashion imagery chosen for the video included a leotard made out of plastic yellow flowers. 'I was talking to somebody about how this year in fashion yellow is going to be very big because people are very sad and yellow brings joy like the sun,' she said at the shoot. 'So I'm wearing sunny flowers!'

The next day it was an early start for another gruelling day shooting in a warehouse at the Port of Los Angeles. The inspiration for the 'LoveGame' video was quite different from the sweet 'Eh Eh' – from Little Italy, 'LoveGame' went underground into the New York subway.

The video opened with a particularly raunchy sequence featuring a naked Gaga wearing only body paint and appliqué diamonds, romping with two buff guys, one with 'Love' shaved into his hair, the other with 'Fame' shaved into his hair. The video was set on a subway platform, and featured a troupe of biker-gang dancers who ran through a routine that was heavily influenced by Michael Jackson's 'Bad'.

'I wanted to have that big giant dance video moment,' Gaga explained. 'I wanted it to be plastic, beautiful, gorgeous, sweaty, tar on the floor, bad-ass boys, but when you got close, the look in everybody's eyes was f***ing honest and scary.'

Of course, Gaga had to have some original fashion for the video, which came in the shape of glasses that looked like a chain-link fence. 'I love the imagery of a downtown, bad-ass kid walking down the street with his buddies, grabbing a pair of pliers and making a pair of sunglasses out of a fence on the street,' she commented.

'I thought that imagery was so real, and it shows that no matter who you are, or where you come from, or how much money you have in your pocket, you're nothing without your ideas. Your ideas are all you have. The opening of the video is me with this chain-link hood and these intense glasses. They look so hard. It looks like I plied them right out of the fence and put them on my face.'

The video of 'LoveGame' had plenty of shock factor: the

nakedness at the start, the raunchy dancing, and also the scene when Gaga pushes a cop into an elevator. Alternating shots in the elevator feature Gaga dancing and tonguing a male cop, then a female cop, and it caused quite a ruckus when it was released a few months later.

The days of filming had been fairly intensive, but Gaga still managed to find herself a little love interest on the shoot of 'LoveGame', where she met Speedy, an LA-based model and entrepreneur who the feisty singer became quite fond of as they worked.

Unfortunately for Gaga, though, there was no time for romance. With the video shoots wrapped, Gaga and her ever-increasing tour entourage headed for Britain, where the Pussycat Dolls tour was about to commence in Scotland.

Gaga flew into London on 12 January to work on material in the studio and do some promotion with the British media for her album. Anxious to get some snaps of the new chart sensation, the British paps were waiting for her at Heathrow. She had only just got off the plane after the fifteen-hour flight, and was wearing a bra and PVC trousers. She wasn't expecting a crowd of photographers sticking huge cameras in her face – the last time she had been in the UK, no one knew who she was!

At first she was a little frosty to the pushy paps, but it didn't take long for Gaga's charismatic knack for showing-off to kick into gear. Once it did, she posed for pictures and chatted to a couple of the photographers before being whisked away to spend some time in the studio, soaking up the British vibe.

Despite the cold weather and the rain, Gaga refused to cover up, even picking up some fish and chips on the way to the studio one night dressed only in black leggings, a green leotard, leather jacket and shades. The paps loved Gaga and followed her everywhere. The British public couldn't wait to see what zany outfit she was going to wear next, and she didn't disappoint them, wearing everything from sequinned panties to a black latex corset with open-toed latex boots to a white strapless jumpsuit, with no regard for the chilly, damp British winter, and always with her trademark sunglasses on, no matter what time of day it was!

The newspapers particularly loved her hair bows, which had been made for her by fashion designer Christian Siriano, who she'd met at the NowNextNow Awards in 2008. 'Now Gaga turns to Minnie Mouse for inspiration!' exclaimed the *Daily Mail*.

Even though she hadn't played any shows in London yet, with high-profile performances on shows like *GMTV* and *T4*, she had the country following her every move.

To warm-up for the Pussycat Dolls' *World Domination* tour, Gaga scheduled a show at G-A-Y, held at Heaven nightclub in London. Wearing nothing but a pair of tight PVC pants and a UV bra, Gaga made her way to the club. The queue for Heaven stretched all the way up to the main road and around the block, a testament to how popular the tiny chick from New York had become over the festive period.

Before taking to the stage, the large screen at the back of the club displayed one of Gaga's *crevettes*, which showed her as Candy Warhol, talking about having her brain removed. The screen counted down from ten to one, and Gaga slinked onto the stage in a shiny, plastic silver dress surrounded by her impossibly fit dancers.

As she performed, she gradually removed parts of her outfit until she was wearing nothing but a black leotard and a new wardrobe item: a metallic breast shield, complete with modelled nipples.

The crowd went crazy for the show, and with almost as many photographers outside as fans inside, Gaga had to be shielded by bodyguards when she was whisked away afterwards. She then headed for Scotland, where the *World Domination* tour was due to start the next night.

Britain's tabloid's loved Gaga instantly. With her sexy lyrics, outlandish outfits and highly stylised videos and live performances, she was perfect media material.

The *Sun* newspaper, amongst others, suggested that the Pussycat Dolls might not be so pleased with the amount of hype that young Gaga had been attracting, and that she might well end up upstaging the girls. 'Lady Gaga looks more like being a headliner' than a support act, the newspaper noted. But if they were feeling insecure about their opening act, the Dolls certainly weren't showing it. They had been looking for a pop performer with some sass to warm up the crowd for their hi-octane show, and the up-and-coming Lady Gaga was the perfect choice for them.

'We're very excited to have Lady Gaga as a special guest on this tour,' they said. 'She is a fresh face, creative, talented and exciting and we can't wait to see the fans dancing to her songs each night.'

Gaga's opening show for the Dolls at the AECC in Aberdeen couldn't have gone better. The arena was already completely packed by the time she got onstage and was full of the fans who had kept 'Just Dance' at number one for a second week, as well as buying enough copies of 'Poker Face' to ensure it entered the charts at number 30 while her album *The Fame* had entered the British album chart at number three.

After a rigorous thirty-minute performance, Gaga stood on the side of the stage to watch the Pussycat Dolls do their thing.

This was their second world tour, and they kept the audience totally entertained with a set filled with motorbikes, heels, glitter, corsets and suspenders.

Like Gaga, the Pussycat Dolls had their origins in the burlesque scene, though they'd abandoned it to embrace being a fully formed pop act.

'I used to go-go dance and set G-strings on fire, stuff like that,' Gaga reminisced when speaking to the *Sun*. 'I've changed my act a little now, but it's definitely still provocative. It began as more of a burlesque show.'

'My father came to see shows when I was in leather thongs and didn't understand,' she explained. 'He couldn't look at me for a few months. But when he saw me getting better, he saw that my ideas were getting stronger. Now my father cries.'

While performing all across the UK with the Pussycat Dolls, Gaga's shows got rave reviews. But she still found herself, more often than not, appearing in the papers because of the outfits she was snapped wearing. Back in London, after two nights at the O2 Arena, Gaga found time to spin some records alongside celebrity producer Mark Ronson at London clubs Punk and The Roxy.

As well as making friends with some of London's musical talent, Gaga ran into Paris Hilton at Punk, where a Nokia party was being held. Not perhaps realising quite how much she had inspired Gaga's album, Paris spent the night posing for photographs and dancing around the DJ booth, while Gaga, assisted by Space Cowboy, played records for a lively crowd.

After the show was over, Mark Ronson – acting as her unofficial tour guide – took Gaga to two exclusive London hotspots Maya and Bungalow 8, before they ended up at a private address in London's East End. Dressed in a black PVC bra and flesh-coloured PVC pencil skirt, Gaga didn't seem bothered about the cold and stayed at the party until 5.30a.m.

As the Pussycat Dolls' tour rolled on through the UK, Gaga's label were busy preparing for her next releases: the EP *The Cherrytree Sessions*, which was about to be released in America, and 'Eh Eh', which was coming out in Australia.

The relentless travelling around Europe with the Dolls, despite being fun, was starting to take its toll on Gaga. She had already played hundreds of shows in 2008, sometimes doing up to four performances a day, but it was only February 2009, and she was already giddy with the number of countries she'd played.

'It's such a bizarre thing going in and out of different countries and different kinds of environments where they know me, or don't know me, or they know the song or they don't know the song – it's unreal,' she confided to the camera in *Transmission Gagavision* episode 29. 'I wake up at four in the morning, and I get on an airplane, and one minute I'm in Germany, the next minute I'm in Sweden, than I'm back in Germany. It's just crazy.'

But it wasn't all bad; even though the touring schedule was tiring, she was starting to realise how much her music had infiltrated countries all around the world. 'It's just so amazing to see how powerful music is. You don't even realise it until you're out here and you're doing it. I was just in the car and my song came on the radio! It's just amazing to see everything finally coming together.' She sighed before pulling herself together and slamming her hand on the table. 'But it's gonna be great! No complaints here!'

One thing that Gaga would never do was complain about

how hard it was to be famous. She had said several times that she knew fame and the music industry was a case of go hard or go home. 'It's required a tremendous amount of heart and faith, and really believing,' she told *Billboard* magazine about her quest for fame. 'I really love what I do so much. I always say that I'm not waiting for some lump of cash and fame so I can buy my beach house – I'm living my dream right now.'

Even though her hectic schedule with the Pussycat Dolls was exhausting her, she was scheduled to have a break soon. At the beginning of March, the Dolls were taking time out from their tour to be the opening act for Britney Spears' *Circus* tour for a couple of months. Gaga would then rejoin the Dolls for the Australian leg of their tour in mid May.

Rather than go home and take a break, though, Gaga had something different in mind. She flew back to LA to get her things ready for her first solo tour, which was just about to kick off.

Chapter Nineteen
The Fame Ball Tour

Gaga, Space Cowboy, her managers Troy and Leah, her troupe of dancers and Dada all stood on the side of the street, looking at the traffic. They had been waiting for about fifteen minutes and there was still no sign. Then suddenly, from around the corner, there it was. A huge, luxury touring coach that pulled up alongside them with its lights flashing.

Gaga was so excited she cheered and clapped, and as she got on the bus she hugged the bemused driver. This was her first ever tour bus for her first ever tour. It had bedrooms in the back with bunk beds, toilets and a shower room. It was a pretty tight squeeze, but the second Gaga laid eyes on her tiny shoe-box of a bedroom, she squealed with joy.

She remembered what it had taken her to get here. All that hard work, all those years and years of playing venues in New York to only a handful of people, getting booed, having beer thrown at her. Now that she was standing on her own tour bus, it seemed like a dream.

The Fame Ball tour, as it was called, was due to kick off at the famous venue the House of Blues in San Diego on 12 March. Behind the scenes, between Gaga, the Haus and all the crew who were working on the tour, The Fame Ball had a more spiritual existence than just a tour. Between themselves they all called the tour Joanne, in memory of Gaga's aunt Joanne, who had died at only nineteen years of age.

Though they had never met, Gaga had always felt very close to her aunt in spirit – her middle name was Joanne too – and she felt like part of the success of *The Fame* was due to her fulfilling some kind of spiritual debt. She thought about Joanne every time she was creating something new, and felt her presence inspiring her.

'I am so mental and sleepless and excited for this tour,' she told *Billboard*. 'This is so different from anything you've seen from me in the past year!'

She wasn't kidding. While Gaga had been touring with the Pussycat Dolls, various members of the Haus back in Los Angeles had been working on new costumes for her to wear onstage, as well as new props and gadgetry for her to wow her audiences with. She had been asked many times by journalists what she planned to do on The Fame Ball tour, but she had kept her mouth tightly shut, knowing that they'd all go crazy when they saw.

Touring with the Dolls had been a great chance for Gaga to plan what she wanted to achieve on her own headline tour. And now the time had come, she wasn't restricted by time, space or even money (to a certain degree).

Apart from a quick group prayer with the Haus before

going onstage, Gaga didn't really have any pre-show rituals. She would drink ginger tea as it was good for her voice, and she even did her own hair and make-up. 'It's funny,' she said in an interview with blogger and broadcaster Buzz Bishop, 'I don't really like anybody to do it for me. So much of my music and who I am is rooted in my vanity, and in that way I don't feel quite like myself, and I don't do it on my own. I sing about fame and good looks and pornography and money – it's kind of a sin if you don't do your own hair and make-up and you sing about sex all day!'

At the House of Blues, once the opening act had finished and the stage had been readied, a huge screen flashed up with one of Gaga's signature *crevettes*. But though they might have seen the film before, the forty-five-minute performance had a whole new collection of risqué outfits and gadgets that wowed the audience.

The Hussein Chalayan bubble dress that she had seen in a museum only months earlier had inspired an installation in her show. She came on stage dressed in a flesh-coloured leotard covered in transparent bubbles, and then played a see-through plastic piano that was also filled with transparent bubbles!

She alternated outfits throughout the show, changing into a sculpted prom dress and peep-toe boots, as well as the origami dress she had become famous for in 2008.

And if casual spectators thought Gaga's outfits were outrageous, there were shows where she was almost upstaged by the fans. Die-hard Team Gaga spared no effort when getting ready to see their pop icon. Every show she played, the audience was a sea of colour, with club kids all dolled up in fur, face paint, wigs, Mardi Gras masks and beads, leotards and their own 'couture' costumes.

'I really love it when I see that my music and my fashion is affecting pop culture,' Gaga told *iProng*. 'That makes me feel famous. It's much more important to see young girls wearing shoulder pads ... or having their hair in a different way, or speaking differently or using new words or listening to music in a genre that they've never maybe tapped into before, that to me is what fame is. It's inspiring music to be less lazy.'

Gaga remembered when she'd first started out, reading all the comments about her on blogs, which either thought she was the real deal or thought she was trying too hard. In reality, it was a mixture of both. Gaga did work hard, sacrificing sleep, food and love to work her punishing routine of travelling, performing, designing new clothes for her shows and writing music constantly.

'I don't wake up in the morning and think I'm too good to do an interview, or too good to write a new song, or too cool to play a show for a small stage,' she said. 'I do anything and everything because I really, really love what I do.'

Unusually for her, Gaga was also finding time to fit a little love into her life. She had kept in touch with Speedy since meeting him on the 'LoveGame' shoot back in January. As she was spending so much time in Europe, the pair remained friends at first, but now that she was back in America, they had met up again and started dating. Friends said they were inseparable, and they were spotted out at dinner by the paps on numerous occasions during the first leg of The Fame Ball tour.

If Gaga had cared to look, there was plenty of other commentary about her in the newspapers, including haters who just wanted to do her down. In an interview with the *Daily Star*, The Rakes front man Alan Donohoe said, 'Lady Gaga is trash and dresses like a prostitute. I think she's terrible and really ugly. I hate her.'

Given that The Rakes had released a new album only the week before, everyone knew his words were simply an attempt to steal some headlines and sell some records, and it was a cheap trick.

There were also plenty of people ready to heap praise on Gaga, including Ne-Yo, another opening act for the Pussycat Dolls. 'I have never been so excited about an artist before,' he told the *Daily Star*. 'Lady Gaga has it all. Being yourself is what makes an artist. You should nurture what you've got. She epitomises to me what artistry is. She is a strange one, but it's refreshing. She makes no apologies for being who she is. She takes pride in being an individual and I made it my business to tell her when we met up on the road.'

The opening night of The Fame Ball tour was a massive hit. Any first-night nerves disappeared, and The Fame Ball rolled on to Los Angeles and the Wiltern Theater, where a whole host of celebrities, hangers-on and wannabes turned up to see what all the fuss was about, including Clique Girlz, Mika, Kelly Osbourne, Raven Symone, LeAnn Rimes and none other than the king of innovative, electronic hip hop, Kanye West.

Gaga finished up her performance and began to walk offstage, only to be surprised by her friend Perez Hilton, who walked on with a microphone wearing a hair bow and wouldn't let her leave. He had a special award to present to her for 'Just Dance', which had sold over three million copies worldwide!

Gaga was choked up as she accepted the award, and all her dancers and Space Cowboy rallied around her as tears streamed down her face. Also onstage were her label boss Vincent Herbert, who she gave a tearful thanks to for discovering her, and her manager Troy Carter, who she high-fived.

'I f***ing love you!' she called out to the audience and her screaming fans as she finally walked offstage.

It was a night for celebration. And as The Fame Ball rolled a glittery, sequined path through America in March, it only served to confirm Gaga's status as pop music royalty. Every night was a sell-out, and fans would line up around the block outside venues in case perhaps a few tickets were available on the door.

Back in the UK, fervent fans were keeping Gaga at the top of both the album and the singles chart. *The Fame* had been released in January, had charted at number three and had only managed to stay in the top ten since then. But this week it climbed to the number one spot, alongside single 'Poker Face', which was number one in the singles chart!

Achieving the top spot in both charts in the UK was notoriously rare – the last artist who had managed it was Duffy in 2008, with album *Rockferry* and single 'Mercy'. Gaga had not only repeated that success, but 'Just Dance' was the biggest selling single of the year so far in Britain, having sold more than 550,000 copies!

Gaga's success also lead to a bit of spotlight stealing by her new 'friend' Paris Hilton. Even though the two had only hung out backstage at a party in London in January, Paris was now evidently borrowing from Gaga's style in order to get a piece of the publicity action. First she turned up for a photo shoot in Malibu in futuristic shades and a dominatrix outfit with her hair cut into a bob and straight fringe. Then a couple of days later, when filming her reality TV show *British Best Friend* in Venice Beach, Paris again turned up wearing Gaga-inspired threads: a black corset, stripper heels and a beehive hairdo. The similarities were uncanny and led many newspapers and fashion blogs to accuse Paris of stealing Gaga's style.

In fact, Gaga had noticed Paris being 'influenced' by her look nearly a year previously, when the LA socialite had turned up dressed all in black, with a headband and bright red lipstick.

'Get your own style hilly,' Gaga had posted on her blog on 1 August 2008. 'We know you might be getting some tips from your rocked bf, but next time you want to be bad ass, don't wear a headband.'

Back in the UK, Gaga's explosion into the charts was also ringing bells with a certain Scottish producer. Calvin Harris checked his emails and, sure enough, found an email that had been sent to him on 1 January 2008, asking him to work with her.

'I thought, "Lady Gaga", what sort of name is that' he said to the *Sun*. 'So I replied saying, "Nah, I'm not into that." Fast forward a year and she's the biggest thing.'

Harris claimed he didn't regret turning her down, as he didn't think the song he heard then was that good, but he must have been smarting from the decision. He was looking into working with Katy Perry, but it was obvious that Gaga was going to be a bigger star than Perry, so Harris must have been kicking himself.

Gaga had no time to worry about such matters. Along with the record label, she was preparing to shoot the video for the final single from *The Fame*, 'Paparazzi'.

Gaga, Dada and everyone else in the Haus of Gaga had been working on the treatment for 'Paparazzi' for months. Rather than just a music video, they envisaged a short film.

Gaga had painstakingly drawn out storyboards for the video, examining every frame and detail.

Finally she had the level of creative control she'd wanted over a video – and it was for her favourite song from *The Fame*. To help guide the video in the right direction, Swedish director Jonas Åckerlund was hired. Having worked on big concept videos for Smashing Pumpkins and Madonna, Jonas had enough experience to ensure the video would live up to Gaga's expectations.

The plot line for the video featured Gaga with Swedish actor Alexander Skarsgård as her boyfriend. Gaga is a starlet constantly hounded by photographers. Her boyfriend takes her out onto the balcony to kiss, but she sees paparazzi in the bushes. She tries to get her boyfriend to stop, but when he won't she realises he has invited the paps there to take pictures. She smashes a bottle over his head and he throws her off the balcony in a scene that pays homage to Alfred Hitchcock's film *Vertigo*.

With Gaga injured from the fall, the headlines proclaim her career is over. However, she makes a recovery from her accident and gets back together with her boyfriend, who she then poisons in order to get back in the headlines.

The video ends with Gaga posing for her mug shots as if they were paparazzi shots. 'I don't know if you remember the photos of Paris Hilton and Nicky Hilton and Lindsay Lohan with coke on their nose. Those girls were my inspiration. I was reading tabloids as if they were textbooks. This also has a bit of a Courtney Love vibe to it. There's an art to fame. I get inspiration from all over. That is what inspired the "Paparazzi" video,' she told a journalist in Manila.

The video for 'Paparazzi' was full of references to other

sources: as well as Lindsay Lohan et al, it was a combination of film noir, Cindy Sherman, cyborgs, *Macbeth* and horror films of the 1950s, which Gaga was becoming increasingly obsessed with.

Long-time pal and Haus member Laurie-Ann Gibson was given the task of choreographing the eight-minute video, while Jonas Åckerlund's wife, Bea – an honorary member of the Haus – was charged with styling it. Gaga and Bea had met before *The Fame* was released, and Gaga had wanted Bea to work on all her videos, but Bea had just given birth and wasn't ready to go back to work at the time. For this video, however, which her husband Jonas was directing, it was perfect timing for Bea to get involved as Gaga's personal stylist.

'She's like a sister that I never had,' Bea told *Anthem* magazine about her relationship with Gaga. 'She never had a personal stylist before me, but she has a creative director named Matthew Williams [Dada] that she works with that does all the set design and collaborates with her on all her own designs. She hasn't really worked with one particular stylist before me.'

The video included a number of different looks, including a number of Thierry Mugler archive pieces, Dior, Tom Binns, Giuseppe Zanotti, Dolce & Gabbana, Betony Vernon for Swarovski Runway Rocks, Chanel, Boudicca and Boy London. The list of designers whose work was featured in the video was as long as Gaga's arm, but her favourite look of the shoot was the Thierry Mugler robot. When it arrived, it was in a huge metal box with padlocks on it, which was really exciting for Gaga and the Haus!

For the scene at the start, Gaga wore a number of diamond bracelets from Loree Rodkin, which were worth about $100,000. Bea designed the wheelchair herself, exchanging the wheels for low riders, ordering Gucci fabric and embellishing it with Swarovski crystals. Originally, she made a metal logo that read 'Gaga' which fixed onto the wheels, but she ended up changing it for the Chanel logo.

The expense of the 'Paparazzi' video was a long way from the humble beginnings of the girl from the Lower East side who'd embellished three-dollar bras to get the sparkly look. Now she was dripping with real diamonds.

Unfortunately, there were certain parts of the video shoot that didn't go down too well with Gaga's squeeze, Speedy. At the start of the shoot, the pair were spotted kissing on set and smooching all over each other at a sushi restaurant in Los Angeles the following evening. But according to RadarOnline, Speedy was fuming after a particularly hot scene during the shoot. Male triplets from the Swedish band Snake of Eden had been chosen to make out with Gaga on a sofa for one of the scenes. But apparently Speedy got wind of what was happening, walked onto the set while they were shooting and threw a fit.

'He started yelling at her,' said a source. 'Not satisfied with screaming at her on the set he followed her into a make-up room and kept berating her.'

As if that drama wasn't enough, there was more video-related bad news for Gaga. Word came to her label from Australia that Network Ten had banned the video for 'LoveGame' due to suggestive footage involving bondage and sexual acts. *Video Hits* also refused to air it during the day, and the video was banned by MTV Arabia. Even back in the US, VH1 and MTV would only play edited versions of the video, where all scenes of Gaga in the nude had been removed.

Gaga couldn't bear all the bad news. The year had been

going so well up until then, but with the end of her relationship with Speedy in sight, and a video that she had spent so long working on being banned, she was in despair. She continued to play dates for The Fame Ball, but her real crowning glory of a TV performance came when she was invited to perform on the *American Idol* results show on 1 April. Her album *The Fame*, which had sold 45,000 copies the week before the show, sold 51,000 copies the week the show aired and 56,000 copies the week after.

That same week, the single 'Poker Face' hit the number one spot in America on the Billboard Hot 100 chart, making Gaga the first artist in almost ten years – and only the fourth artist in twenty-five years – to have her first two singles reach number one in America.

Even though her records were riding high in the charts, Gaga was desperate to escape from The Fame Ball for a short while and recover from her broken heart, so she headed to the UK for a week of publicity.

Chapter Twenty
Escape From LA

Despite her heartache and the 'LoveGame' video troubles, Gaga still found time and energy to update her appearance often enough to give the paparazzi a headache. As she boarded a plane in Los Angeles, bound for London, she was photographed with her trademark short, peroxide blonde bob. But by the time she landed in London some ten hours later, she was sporting a different look: long platinum-blonde hair with pink highlighted extensions.

The very next day, the singer emerged from Blakes hotel, where she was staying, with a teacup and saucer in hand and her whole head dyed purple!

The day after that she appeared on *Friday Night With Jonathan Ross*, with her peroxide blonde bob back and looking totally fierce. Ross seemed totally bemused by the twenty-three-year-old, and didn't seem to know how to relate to her. He was obviously confused by her crazy outfits and brash outspo-kenness – she told him she would make love to her old boyfriend and think about women sometimes – but more than anything he couldn't understand her choice of drink.

'I was talking to the members of the Haus about the power of image and the camera, and I wanted to say something on a real level about fame,' she later told *Billboard* magazine. 'I drink a lot of tea, and I decided to take a purple teacup out of my china collection, then take it to London and make it famous. I put it in videos and had fans pose with it and put it on TV – at one point, the teacup had a call time.'

As she sipped her ginger tea throughout the show, it was clear that Ross had no idea how to relate to her – or her teacup. When asked about the comment that Christina Aguil-era had made – that she didn't know whether Gaga was a man or a woman – Gaga deadpanned back to him, 'I do have a re-ally big donkey dick.' It was a comment that would come back to haunt her after her Glastonbury performance later that summer.

Gaga's lukewarm appearance on *Friday Night With Jonathan Ross* was a bit of a disappointment to her fans. However, they were in for a treat when she was interviewed by Paul O'Grady. Better known for many years as the cross-dressing Lily Savage, Paul was obviously much better acquainted with Gaga's bur-lesque, musical theatre background, and their interview was far more lively. Gaga even gave O'Grady her hair bow to wear, to many whoops and cheers from the audience.

She even gave him an insight into her creative team, the mysterious Haus of Gaga. 'They're my friends,' she said. 'They're all very young and they work with me on designing the show and putting the music and the fashion and the dance and lighting altogether. I've met a few really amazing people in this business, and the thing they've all said to me is don't let anyone take your creative people away from you, so I don't get caught up in all the hype and start working with all the really huge people. I keep my close friends really near me and we keep making the same stuff that we were making in New York four years ago.'

O'Grady also revealed a little more about her rider – saying that she had the fewest requests of any guest he had ever had on the show. She didn't want any liquor – no beer or wine – she just wanted hummus!

'Everybody thinks I'm plastered out of my mind all the time onstage, but the truth is that I'm pretty militant about rehearsal,' she said to him. 'I'm bossy, but I just want to do a good job!'

Her teacup made another appearance at the Radio One studios in central London. She had carried it everywhere with her on her publicity stint in the UK – even taking it into restaurants with her. In fact, there was almost a Gaga emergency when she misplaced it at one point, accidentally leaving it in London's Nobu restaurant. She even sent a black cab to the restaurant to collect it once she realised what she had done.

British newspapers were beside themselves trying to keep up with her antics, even calling her label for comment on the teacup. They received a well-considered response from the Haus of Gaga: 'Lady Gaga does not want to reveal anything about the teacup itself, but drinking ginger tea is very good for singers.'

Gaga's on-board makeover and her eccentricity with her famed teacup delighted her British fans, as did her frequent appearances at London nightspots in ever more outrageous outfits. She enjoyed drinks at the Groucho club, then headed for Bungalow 8, a nightclub that Mark Ronson had introduced her to on her last visit to the city, wearing a see-through chiffon catsuit with black electrical tape across her nipples – a burlesque fashion, called nipple pasties.

Even though it was the dead of night, she was still wearing her trademark sunglasses and hair bow, and when faced with the crowd of photographers she decided to play them at their own game. She whipped out her Nikon camera and took pictures of the paparazzi, before getting in the car that was waiting for her and speeding away.

Determined to stay one step ahead of the paps, she turned up for a radio interview at Capital Radio wearing a black pirate hat and sunglasses. She might have been wearing trousers this time, but she still had her beloved teacup and saucer with her. 'My teacup is so famous,' she commented. 'I yelled at her today – I said, "You're stealing my thunder, go to bed!" You know now it's a gimmick and it's just my teacup. That's my teacup that I like to take everywhere; it makes me feel at home. It's become a celebrity. I miss home sometimes and I drink a lot of tea, so instead of drinking from paper I ask for china.'

It had been a packed week, but Gaga managed to squeeze in some socialising when she went for dinner with an artist she'd been interested in working with: Mika. Dressed in a pair of cream thigh-high lace-up PVC boots, black PVC pants and bra, an oversized black hat and with her lips painted geisha style, Gaga and Mika headed to Hakkasan in central London for dinner.

With the newspapers going crazy over her outfits, Gaga refused to be drawn into wearing anything less provocative.

'These boots were made for walking,' she wrote on Twitter after her meal with Mika.

If she had shocked people in London, it was nothing compared to how shocked the media were with her behaviour in Moscow. At a press conference before *The Fame Ball* rolled into Moscow, people gasped at Gaga's outspoken comments, which included statements like, 'I like pornography … I love gays … my grandmother likes to look at my legs when I'm dancing.'

At the concert in Moscow, she continued to shock by telling her crowd, 'There's only one thing I love more than drinking and that's money, honey! I hope that everyone gets drunk tonight, and then go home and have sex!'

It was a little too much for the conservative Russian police, who almost arrested her the day after the show. Dressed in a leather leotard, she posed for pictures in Moscow's Red Square, but her raunchy attire caught their attention and two policeman ran over to her.

'I was having a little photo shoot and all of a sudden the police came out of nowhere and clapped their fingers,' she said to the *Sun*. 'I think it means whore in Russian.'

'They tried to arrest me in Russia, for leather at St. Basil's. But all is calm in the red square, as I leave the east, Paris bound' Gaga commented on Twitter about the run-in with the Russian police.

Though the Russian police might not have approved of her outfit, all over the world Gaga wannabes were putting on leotards and raunching up their performances. Back in the UK, Girls Aloud member and *X Factor* judge Cheryl Cole took to the stage at a Girls Aloud gig in Sheffield dressed in nothing but a skimpy, high-cut leotard.

Towards the end of April, Gaga made a couple more stops

to play some more shows in Europe, but all was not well in Camp Gaga. Still hurting over her break-up with Speedy, she was pining for him and wondering why she never had any luck when it came to men.

'I am totally confident that I am an incredible artist and performer,' she confided in the *Sun* newspaper. 'I am extremely confident about my body, the way I dress, the way I want to look, but I have no confidence when it comes to men. Men are a disaster area for me.'

'It's so weird,' she added. 'I believe I am super sexy. I believe I am incredible, but I have absolutely no luck with boyfriends.'

With her heart painfully broken, she boarded the plane back to America, getting ready to press on with *The Fame Ball* tour. The first few shows were in her beloved New York, and she was excited about seeing her friends again. As she landed, a text message came through; it was Speedy, and he was flying to New York to see her. Within hours they had made up, and were papped walking hand in hand through the leafy streets of Manhattan.

Gaga caused quite a commotion at a store in Queens shortly after returning to New York when she turned up in a transparent bodysuit, with only a bra and thong to cover her modesty, in order to buy some tortellini to cook a meal for Speedy's parents. The move didn't go down well with her beau, who suggested, 'Why don't you have a fuckin' meet-and-greet in the frozen-foods aisle?'

It was a star-studded show. Gaga had invited all her New York art friends like Lady Starlight to come and join *The Fame Ball* tour for a few shows, and they all stared in amazement at the thousands of people packed into Terminal 5, including a number of celebrities who had shown up to watch. Cyndi Lauper, Stephen Klein and Zac Posen were all hanging out in the VIP boxes. Even more exciting for Gaga, Madonna was backstage, with boyfriend Jesus and her daughter Lourdes!

'I was very humbled that Madonna came to the show,' Gaga told *MTV News*. 'I had been hearing all week that she was going to come, and I was like, "Oh, OK," and I didn't want to talk about it or tell anyone because I thought it was kind that she would want to come at all.'

Madonna's daughter Lourdes – evidently a big Gaga fan – was dressed like a true member of Team Gaga that night, in neon-green leggings and monochrome brogues, and she danced throughout the show. Madonna and Lourdes managed to slip out unnoticed at the end of the show, which Gaga was pleased about, fearing that if the crowd had seen her they might have trampled her. The show was a great success, and Gaga was delighted that pop royalty like Madonna had taken time out of her busy schedule to come and see her.

'When Madonna came to my show, she didn't have to come,' Gaga said later. 'She knows that when she shows up it affects the way that people perceive me. I always think that people that are like that are real class acts. That's really nice of them, they don't have to do that.'

As well as Madonna turning up to see her perform, Gaga's New York show inspired some spontaneous lovemaking in the crowd. 'My sister texted me and she was like, "Madonna is fifteen feet away from me. And there are two guys having sex in the audience." I just remember thinking, Wow, this is exactly what I wanted. I've got Madonna and I've got gay sex!' she told *V* magazine.

*

After the show, to celebrate, Gaga donned an all-in-one, see-through maroon chiffon bodysuit, nipple pasties and towering wedge heels to party with boyfriend Speedy at a club in Manhattan.

There was a lot to celebrate. 'Just Dance' had just been certified platinum in America, and Gaga had appeared on *Dancing With the Stars* and *The Ellen DeGeneres Show*. Appearing on *Ellen* was a particular honour for Gaga, as Ellen was a pioneer of the modern gay rights movement in America, a cause close to Gaga's heart.

Of course, she made sure her outfit was as outrageous as it could be for the show, wearing an all-in-one denim patchwork jumpsuit – going against her 'no pants' policy – but on her head she wore an incredible orbiting headpiece made by London designer Nasir Mazhar. 'Are you in braces?' joked the host.

Gaga didn't let Ellen get many words in before blurting out, 'I love you so much. You're such an inspiration to women, and to the gay community … it means more to me to be on this show than anywhere.'

Even though Gaga performed a spectacular version of 'Poker Face' on the show – half acoustic standing on the stool and playing her piano bending down, and half electronic with all her dancers – it was again her outfit, in particular the headgear, that stole the headlines.

A couple of days later, Gaga was joined by a reporter from *Rolling Stone*, who was due to spend a couple of days with the Lady on tour, in preparation for writing a story about her to grace the cover of the magazine's June issue.

'I like doing this all the time,' she told the reporter. 'It's my passion. When I'm not doing a show, I'm writing a song, or I'm on the phone with Dada yapping about a hemline. The truth is, the psychotic woman that I truly am comes out when I'm not working. When I'm not working, I go crazy!'

Speedy was also travelling with Gaga on this part of the tour, as was her celebrity buddy, Perez Hilton. But despite this, Gaga was still down on herself about her love life, remembering how badly she'd been hurt when she had broken up with Lüc.

'Speedy means a lot to me,' she said of her current squeeze. 'But my music's not going to wake up tomorrow morning and tell me it doesn't love me any more. So I'm content with my solitude. I'm OK with being alone. I choose to have someone in my life when I can.'

The following Monday, *Rolling Stone* had arranged for the photo shoot for the cover of the magazine, where she appeared dressed in a transparent plastic corset with frizzy hair and geisha lips. The photo shoot turned out to be a star-studded event, with Cyndi Lauper and Marilyn Manson showing up to say hi. In traditional shocking style, Manson was carrying a glass of absinthe – illegal in America – and being filmed on a hand-held camcorder by his assistant.

In her dressing room, Gaga was giving a sneak peek of the finished 'Paparazzi' video. At the start of the video, where she makes out with her on-screen boyfriend, Manson leaned over to her and said, much to the horror of the *Rolling Stone* journalist, 'I want to be that guy. I want to be balls deep.'

Gaga laughed off Manson's advances, but he tried again, pointing to a coat hanger and saying, 'You're going to need these for the abortion later. I'll give you a cervical exam.' Gaga continued to laugh him off, but as well as trying to pick her up, Manson was a big fan of Gaga's work.

'She knows exactly what she's doing,' he said. 'She's very smart, she's not selling out, she's a great musician, she's a great singer, and she's laughing when she's doing it, the same way that I am.'

Also present on the photo shoot were Gaga's parents, Joseph and Cynthia. Dad Joseph was sporting a new Gaga lightning-bolt tattoo, while mum Cynthia wore a Gaga lightning-bolt necklace. As they watched their daughter prance and pose for the camera, they couldn't have been prouder of what she had achieved.

After a successful trip across America, Gaga packed up her fame ball and got ready for the long flight to Australia, where she was set to rejoin the Pussycat Dolls for the Australian leg of their *World Domination* tour. The seventeen-hour flight from Los Angeles to Sydney was the longest time Gaga had spent on her own for six months – the rest of the time she'd been crammed in a tour bus with ten other people. She took advantage of the time out, and because she usually averaged only five hours' sleep a night, she was really excited about sleeping for the whole flight.

When she got off the plane in Sydney, she was expecting to go to her car relatively unnoticed, but instead she got a big flashy welcome. She found the paparazzi in the city really similar to London: pushy, in your face, and they seemed to appear everywhere she went.

The Australian media were predictably confounded when she turned up for interviews in her normal clothes – which for Gaga consisted of leotards, corsets, hot pants and knee-high boots. 'The biggest misconception about me is I'm a character or a persona,' she said to the *Sydney Morning Herald*. 'That when the lights and cameras turn off, I turn into a pumpkin. It's simply not true. I make music and art and design all day long. Yes, I wash my face and go to sleep, but when I wake up, I am always Lady Gaga.'

As Gaga's popularity had increased so much since the start of the year, the tabloids tried to start rumours about how the Dolls were fuming at Gaga's new notoriety, annoyed that she was going to upstage them. But this was just untrue media hype. The Dolls denied all the tabloid allegations and Gaga backed them up, stating that they all got on well on tour.

'I don't feel that way about the Pussycat Dolls,' she said to an Australian fan. 'I love them very much and I'm very grateful to them for having me support them. They've taken me all over the world. I love Nicole [Scherzinger] and they are all so sweet and so sexy. I'm very lucky to be on tour with such humble young women,' she added.

The Australian media was having none of it, though. *The Age* ran a review of her show entitled, 'Fans go gaga as the Lady upstages the Dolls', while the *Herald Sun* proclaimed, 'Lady Gaga upstages Pussycat Dolls at Rod Laver Arena'. The media's and the fans' eyes, it seemed, were focused solely on Gaga. Journalists gushed about her show, particularly her newspaper costume, her entrance on a Vespa and, of course, the bubble installation.

'Part marketing genius, part art project, Gaga proved herself to be an incredible live act,' said *The Age*. 'That made the former burlesque troupe turned pop group the Pussycat Dolls all the more disappointing when they hit the stage and began gyrating to their R&B backing tape … Still, at least they can say that they once supported the great Lady Gaga.'

'For the higher-profile Dolls to charge their (mainly young) fans up to $140 to watch them sing their hits karaoke style without a live band is jaw-dropping,' wrote the *Herald Sun* whilst excusing Lady gaga as 'a young support act' singing live over backing tapes. *The Herald Sun* reporter was clearly not a fan of the Dolls. 'And all their strip-club outfits and strip-club dance moves – complete with poles – couldn't disguise the cheap and nasty production values. Their pyro flames looked more like a cigarette lighter and the video screen imagery was embarrassing.'

Although she was flattered by all the attention, Gaga made sure to pay her dues to the Dolls in every interview, refusing to badmouth them. 'I don't know if anybody knows this or not, but I've never said one bad thing about anybody in the press. Never. And I never will,' she said in an Australian interview. 'And it's because I believe in good artistic karma. It's like, we're all here to support each other, and it doesn't do anybody any good to kick each other.'

Despite this, she would occasionally find her patience tested by pushy radio journalists. In an interview for Nova 96.9 in Brisbane, the only thing the DJ seemed interested in asking Gaga about was how much money she was making, and he didn't listen to her when she told him she was spending all her money on her live show.

'For the first full year of my career I would do two shows a night always, and I would use the money from the second show to pay for the technology, the stage design of the first show,' she explained when asked for the second time how much she earned.

'But now I'm starting to make money, since I don't care about money, I spent everything that I make on my show. I'm not rolling around with Range Rovers or Rolls Royces, I have impressive costumes and a stage show.'

Still the presenter wouldn't give up. Wasn't she investing it all for her future, in some nice high-interest bank account somewhere?

There was a second silence as Gaga composed herself before saying, 'Maybe I don't have the same priorities as all the pop singers that everybody knows about – buying fancy cars and big houses and flaunting their wealth. I don't care about those things. I care about my show.'

It had been a stressful interview. To add to her worries, back in the US the 'Paparazzi' video had been leaked onto the Internet weeks before it was due to the shown! Gaga was furious. She had spent so long working on the video, and now the grand unveiling had been taken away from her. She took to Twitter to retaliate: 'Stop leaking my motherf***ing videos.'

Due to the leak, Gaga decided the best thing to do was act quickly. She called her friend Perez Hilton back in Los Angeles, and asked if she could release the video early on his blog. The video premiered there and drew thousands of views from fans all over the world.

Despite her problems with the press and her video, she managed to get through her visit to Australia relatively unscathed, and enjoyed the rest of her time there. The tour had been gruelling to say the least, so one of Gaga's childhood friends – who she had known since she was four years old – flew out to Australia to spend a few days with her, and they had a fun time sight-seeing, even finding time to go to the zoo and hold a wombat.

Despite her friend's visit, Gaga was exhausted and in need of some time off, so her label gave her and the rest of her performers a well-deserved week's break. Rather than going home to see her family, though, Gaga hopped on a plane to Hawaii, with the paparazzi hot on her heels.

Chapter Twenty-One **A Romantic Getaway**

Gaga was met at Honolulu airport by model boyfriend Speedy, who was waiting for her with a bunch of flowers. Bystanders saw the two embrace, before they hopped into a waiting car and sped off to their hotel.

Even in Hawaii they weren't alone. Though they snuck off to a secluded pebble beach, the paparazzi followed them there, where they caught some shots of the princess of pop in downtime mode, wearing a black bikini, long black-shirt and flip flops.

Gaga, however, had only one thing on her mind – getting some loving from her man.

Just before leaving Australia, there had been rumours that due to her gruelling tour schedule she had ended their relationship, saying she had no time for a man in her life. But they certainly seemed to be having fun together in Hawaii. Speedy then flew with her to Asia, where she played her first dates in Japan, Singapore and Korea.

Back in the US, Gaga's records went from chart strength to strength, with her first single, 'Just Dance', becoming only the fifth song ever to reach the four million mark in paid downloads, while its follow-up, 'Poker Face', was hot on its heels with three million downloads sold. Meanwhile her album *The Fame* reached its fourteenth week in the top 10 on The Billboard 200.

As if that wasn't enough, Kanye West, who had been a huge champion of Gaga's since he saw her perform at Terminal 5 in New York, had a special announcement to make. It was something he and Gaga had been working on in secret – they were planning a tour together. But Gaga wasn't going to be opening for Kanye, and it wasn't planned to be a co-headlining tour. Gaga and Kanye were planning a magnificent live spectacle, which would have the pair performing together as part of one long set.

'She's talented and so incredible that she's not an opening act,' he told MTV. 'We're doing it together, with no opening act.' Kanye called Gaga the new Madonna. He had total faith in her as a songwriter and performer, and he knew their tour was going to blow people's minds.

It was a huge week for Gaga. She celebrated in Japan with a great show, and enjoyed her downtime by eating tons of sushi with her touring crew.

With her three-show tour of Asia over, Gaga headed back to North America, were she was scheduled to perform at the MuchMusic Video Awards in Toronto on 21 June. Even though the video for 'Poker Face' was nominated for International

Video of the Year, no one was more surprised than Gaga when she won. After graciously accepting the award, she didn't have much time before her performance, so ran straight backstage to get ready.

Wanting this live performance to stand out from the others, MuchMusic gave Gaga a huge budget to build an elaborate set, which looked like a futuristic post-apocalyptic world. With a troupe of leather-clad dancers, Gaga entered singing 'LoveGame' and stormed across the stage to the sound of screaming, then went straight into a remixed version of 'Poker Face'.

Gaga had worked and worked on the performance all weekend, rehearsing tirelessly with her dancers and choreographer Laurie-Ann Gibson, and trying out some freaky new costume gadgets that let her fire sparks out of her bra at the end!

'MuchMusic Awards with my best friends,' she said on Twitter. 'The Haus is feverishly at work. It's a long way to the top if you wanna rock'n'roll.'

It might have been a long way for Gaga to get to the top, but now that she was there the crowd were lapping up every second of her show. People went totally ballistic, crying and screaming and chanting for her.

The night had gone really well, but the after party was an event Gaga would always remember. After the awards, all the stars headed to the Cobra nightclub in Toronto, but outside the nightclub there was a confrontation and a fight started. It all happened so quickly it was impossible to see what happened, but someone hit Gaga's friend Perez Hilton in the face.

Ever the peacemaker, Gaga tried to get between them and stop them fighting. 'Guys, come on!' she shouted. 'Come on! We had a beautiful night!'

Unfortunately, her words weren't enough to stop the fight.

Perez thought it was Black Eyed Peas frontman Will.i.am, and took to Twitter with photos of his bloodied face, demanding the police arrest Will. 'I was assaulted by Will.i.am of the Black Eyed Peas and his security guards,' Perez tweeted. 'I am bleeding. Please, I need to file a police report. No joke.'

Just hours later, Will.i.am set up his own Twitter account to tell people what had happened that night. 'Perez Hilton is a liar,' he said in one tweet, then filmed a short video clip to further deny the assault claims.

According to Will.i.am, all the trouble started when Black Eyed Peas singer Fergie asked Perez if he had a problem with her as Perez had said a lot of negative things about her on his blog, not to mention berating Black Eyed Peas' music.

Although Gaga had never suffered from Perez's harsh tongue, he regularly said negative things about celebrities on his blog, which made a lot of them very angry.

Although Gaga was sorry to have witnessed the trouble, she didn't have time to stop as The Fame Ball tour was going back to Europe to play some festivals and some more European dates. First it was back to the UK, where she was scheduled to play Glastonbury Festival, plus some dates as the opening act for reformed British boy band Take That.

The rehearsals for Glastonbury were relentless. They had to take into account many new factors, such as a different stage layout and the unpredictable British weather. This was also Gaga's first show with a live backing band. Even though it looked like it was going to be a dry festival, the site was slick with mud, so Gaga decided on a pair of heeled wellies to ensure she made it onto the stage and through her performance in one piece.

The day before the festival, it was looking like the rehearsals were all done. But something wasn't sitting right with Gaga. Creative director Matt Williams – her Haus member Dada – asked her what it was.

'I want to play a keytar on stage,' said Gaga. 'I have to. Otherwise the performance will be all wrong.'

The stage crew groaned. They were used to last-minute performance changes, but this was taking it to extremes. Dada worked tirelessly to engineer the keytar together, while Gaga worked the changes into the choreography with the dancers. It changed the whole dynamic of the show they had worked so hard to put together, but Gaga was satisfied: it was often last-minute decisions like this one that worked best onstage.

Gaga began her set by emerging from a silver case, which her dancers opened up, singing the song 'Paparazzi'. Dressed in her robot-style sparkly dress, she stood on a rotating platform with the keytar, playing it until the end of the song as the platform rotated, showing her behind to the crowd, which they cheered at. She then ran offstage for a number of costume changes, leaving her backing band to play on. She had almost as many costumes as she did songs, changing into a red latex dress, a black corset, her bubble installation dress and a pink bra during the show.

When she had finished singing 'Boys Boys Boys', Gaga walked to the front of the stage and addressed her fans. 'How are you my little monsters? Are you having a good time?' The crowd screamed as Gaga lay down on the blue Vespa and was pushed across the stage by her burly dancers. 'You know, I was thinking before about my favourite festival experience, because I know exactly how you all feel right now. You're covered in mud, you're sweaty and you smell, but you know what? It's OK. Because what these festivals are all about is suffering for your love of music!'

After another costume change, Gaga brought out the spark-throwing bra she had worn at the MuchMusic Awards in Toronto, shooting fire from her boobs during the chorus of 'Eh Eh'. She then finished her show with the famous bubble installation while singing 'Poker Face'.

Gaga caused an absolute storm and inspired British pretenders to the pop princess throne to increase the outrageousness of their own outfits in a bid to keep up. Londoner Lily Allen took to the stage in a revealing jumpsuit and pink wig, but it wasn't a patch on Gaga's wardrobe.

Behind the scenes, however, there was only sadness. Tragically, one of Gaga's heroes – Michael Jackson – had passed away just before the festival started. Beside herself with grief, she scrapped all interviews before her Glastonbury début and spent hours on the phone to producer RedOne back in America. According to the *Sun* newspaper, 'Gaga was hysterical with grief. She could not be consoled and spent the day on the phone to her producer RedOne in America. They penned hits "Poker Face" and "Just Dance" together. He had been working with Michael on new material recently and was beside himself.'

Gaga was so stricken with grief that, despite being sensational at Glastonbury, she couldn't pull herself together to fulfil the support slot on Take That's tour, collapsing with exhaustion backstage, according to the *Mirror*. Even though her official reason was illness, rumours spread that she couldn't perform because she was so upset about Michael Jackson's death. 'I truthfully don't know what world I'm making music in any more without Michael,' she said later in an interview in Germany.

Gaga's label put out a statement saying that she was feeling unwell on Saturday and, after consulting her doctor, decided that she was unable to perform with Take That at Old Trafford. The statement also said that Gaga was resting on doctor's orders, but would be rejoining Take That at Wembley the following weekend.

Gary Barlow was incredibly annoyed at Gaga's decision, not least because she had managed to do a sound check before deciding she couldn't perform! 'Don't get me started. You should have heard me backstage,' he said to the fans.

After resting up for a whole day in bed, Gaga couldn't sit still a second longer. She was up and out, doing more charity work, this time for Orange RockCorps, where Gaga joined fifty youngsters at a Manchester support centre for people affected by HIV. Swapping her microphone for a paintbrush, Gaga helped the other volunteers turn a bare car park into a lush vibrant garden, which would be open to anyone living with, or affected by, HIV. In exchange for their time, volunteers got tickets to exclusive concerts. The Manchester volunteers got tickets to see Gaga perform at the Manchester Apollo later in the month.

In typical Gaga style, the chick from New York brought a lot of attention to the Manchester project, mainly because of her outfit, which included a large button-shaped hat made out of hair.

But it wasn't all roses in the Gaga garden. After collapsing with exhaustion before the Take That concert, those close to her feared she was heading for a breakdown. The rumour mill said Gaga was headed for rehab, but in reality, just a couple of days later she was spotted drinking at the Lowry Hotel bar, which apparently didn't go down too well with the boys in Take That.

Gaga's presence in the UK was causing quite a media stir, with the tabloids seizing the opportunity to cash in whenever they could. Kelly Osbourne was quoted in the *Mirror* by their 3a.m. girls as saying, 'She's a butter face. She has everything but the face. She reminds me of Peaches Geldof. I love Lady Gaga's tracks, but I just wish she'd keep her mouth shut. She talks way too much and has too much attitude. It's starting to make me go off her.'

Poor Kelly was distraught when she saw the quote on the Internet the next day, and spoke to Gaga's pal Perez Hilton to put things right. 'I have a big mouth and that's no secret,' she said. 'I often say things that get me into trouble, but I always stand by them, BUT when words are being put into my mouth and things are being printed that I did not say it really makes me really mad. I am a huge fan of Lady Gaga. If anything I'm slightly jealous of her wardrobe and I am definitely in no position to be calling anyone a butter face.'

Luckily for Kelly, as always, Gaga was too gracious to respond to any alleged comments about her. She was also too busy. While in London, she played two shows as the opening act for Take That at Wembley Stadium, with no issues about performing this time. She also took time out from her hectic schedule to take lessons from the Queen of Pop, turning up to Madonna's show to watch one of her heroes perform.

She also did a couple of risqué photo shoots for *Maxim* and *V* magazine, and even made a little baby Gaga suit for her producer RedOne, whose partner had just had a baby. However, she wouldn't spill any details about the tour with Kanye West, only stating that it would be one of the most important moments in music ever. 'I truthfully adore Kanye,' she added. 'I always poke fun at him and joke around. We have a lovely creative relationship. He's so sweet. I can't say enough good things. He's undeniably brilliant.'

Although there were rumours romantically linking Gaga and Kanye, she was keen on keeping their relationship purely professional. Having been hurt so badly in love before, there was no way Gaga was going to risk their friendship. In her opinion, her perfect man was the unattainable dead composer Beethoven! And even though she was seeing Speedy, she never referred to him as her boyfriend.

'I'm a single girl. I like to have a good time,' she said, then added jokingly, 'I just sleep with the guys in the band all the time because it's easier.' Even though she was physically attracted to women, Gaga had never been in love with a woman. But all her boyfriends had had incredibly negative reactions to lesbian leanings. 'The fact that I'm into women, they're all intimidated by it,' she told *Rolling Stone*. 'It makes them uncomfortable. They're like, "I don't need to have a threesome, I'm happy with just you".'

Gaga also spoke to the *Mirror* about her addiction to buying more and more incredible outfits and gadgetry for her stage show.

'I've gone bankrupt about four times now. My manager wants to shoot me,' she joked. 'Every dollar I earn goes on the show. Now we're finally getting to a place where it's not bankruptcy. Then again, with another tour coming up soon I'll probably be homeless again!'

With a number of high-profile events planned for the summer, Gaga and the Haus were busy creating more outrageous outfits and doing everything they could to ensure she was the only word on everyone's lips.

Chapter Twenty-Two Fashion and Music

After playing so many shows, Gaga could finally realise her dream of creating crazy couture and wearing a different outfit almost every day of the week. In July, she upped the ante with yet more outrageous costumes, and as a result was in the news almost every day.

She performed at the *Isle of MTV* in Malta, but it wasn't the performance that got people talking; it was what she wore to the press conference held for the show. It was a slinky, studded black leather dress - not particularly remarkable for Gaga. What was remarkable was the black face mask - not unlike a gimp mask - that finished off the outfit. She always knew how to grab people's attention.

There were gasps from the journalists as she walked into the room and sat down. It seemed like she couldn't quite see where she was going, and no one could see her face. Afterwards conspiracy theories abounded that it wasn't even Gaga under the mask, though there was no one else in the world of pop with the audacity to turn up to a press conference without their face showing.

In Denmark she turned up to an autograph signing wearing a huge purple beehive on her head, accessorized by a flesh-coloured leotard and white blazer. While in Paris she was spotted wearing a latex A-line skirt, bra and carrying an umbrella, even though it wasn't raining. 'In Paris, coffee and cigarettes looking through Jean-Paul Gautier's show and salivating like a starved fashion gangster,' she said about the French capital on Twitter. '*C'est genial.* xxox.'

Back in the UK, Gaga was always one step ahead of the British paparazzi with her fashion choices. Her manager had told her to be especially careful of the British paps, as they were known for being more ruthless and invasive than the press in almost any other country. From her days gogo dancing, Gaga was used to getting changed anywhere – even underneath tables sometimes – but her manager had warned her always to close the curtains, as you never knew where the British paps might be hiding.

Knowing they would always be following her, she wore increasingly crazy combinations when she was out and about. She was seen in Manchester wearing a cleavage-baring black and pink Jean-Charles de Castelbajac dress and a pair of retro-style sunglasses.

In Hamburg, the first lady of pop made sure everyone knew who she was when she entered a bar after a show wearing only her lingerie. Sources in *Women's Wear Daily* reported that she was very drunk, blowing air kisses and falling over, but winning the love of everyone present by buying them drinks.

Ever devoted to her fans, Gaga even invited some members of Team Gaga backstage at her Cologne show on 17 July. People started queuing outside the Palladium at 9a.m. that morning, determined that by the time the doors opened at 6.30p.m. they would be right at the front. Seeing some very energetic fans going completely crazy throughout her set, she gave them her sunglasses and told her security guards to invite them backstage after the show.

At the end of the show, the burly bouncers pulled four lucky fans over the barriers and led them backstage, where they had to wait twenty minutes. Finally her bodyguards came out to fetch them and took them to her dressing room. Gaga hugged them all and said she didn't normally ask to meet fans after shows, but she had noticed them all going completely mental, and she wanted to thank them for their devotion. She had photos taken with all of them, and told them that yes – as had been rumoured in the press – she was indeed planning to re-release her album *The Fame*, but as an extended release called *The Fame Monster*!

Gaga turned to her manager Troy and said that she really wanted to release some new music soon. She had been touring the same tracks for almost two years – some, three years – and as an artist she was starting to feel like she needed to write more tracks. She didn't want to go stale; she had a need constantly to create.

The experience was obviously weighing on her mind. 'Writing new music today. Monster music,' she wrote on Twitter. 'Take me to the nearest studio, and in coffee shops we'll dream.'

'I'm always writing at some point,' she said to the BBC's *Newsbeat*. 'It starts to take a bit of a backseat just because I'm working on other things but I'm always writing … I'm sure I'll write a few songs in there that I'll give away.'

'When inspiration comes you have to be good at harnessing it and knowing what to do with it,' she says. 'It's all about, "Everyone leave, get out, I need a minute! Every once in a while you've just gotta do for yourself as an artist and make sure that you have your environment conducive to recording a song or writing one.'

Her creative streak was running so hot that it was rumoured she might be asked to appear on a show like *X Factor* or *American Idol* as a talent judge. But Gaga poo-pooed the rumours. She had made her feelings known about shows like that: 'I've never been asked to be a judge, but I wouldn't say yes if I was,' she stated.

'I don't believe it's right to judge music, it's so personal. Right now I'm possessed with this incredible instinctual energy to write joyous melodies. I don't know where it's coming from.'

Gaga's love for her fans knew no bounds. Partly because she was always on the move, her fans were the one thing that remained constant. 'I've been on tour for two years. It's not worth laying out the money for a place,' she told the *News of the World*.

'That's why I gave up my New York apartment. I must admit I feel pretty rootless right now. The only refuge I have is my tour bus. Sometimes I feel that my fans are all that I have. I realised this again recently, when I read a letter from a girl. She wrote to tell me how much she loves me – I just cried.'

From her creative musical streak back to her clothes, Gaga took her fashion consciousness to another level in London to keep the photographers guessing. She was spotted wearing lacy bunny ears and an Alexander McQueen knitted dress with huge black coils that looped around her body.

On another occasion she used her clothing to support charity, by carrying a BBC Children in Need Pudsey bear in her hand while sporting a flowery dress, white gloves and a straw hat. She was even spotted wearing a puffball skirt made from the face of Animal from *The Muppets*.

Her onstage get-ups were also becoming increasingly more elaborate. On 11 July she played one of Britain's biggest festivals, T In The Park, and brought some razzle dazzle to the Scottish audience with mirrorball dresses, beaded slash-front leotards, face masks, energetic dance routines, mopeds and her trademark bubble installation piano.

She had some motivational words for the sun-baked crowd too: 'I know it's crowded, and you're hot and you smell. But you know what you gotta do? Put your hands up and dance, motherfucker!' And with that, she launched into 'Beautiful, Dirty, Rich'.

'What I love most about festivals, because I used to go to them all the time, is that they're an equaliser,' she added. 'Today there's nothing more important than love and music. And tonight, you're gonna spend all your money on food and booze and hookers!'

As well as performing at festivals, Gaga made good on her promise to perform at the Orange RockCorps gig in Manchester, which was a free gig to reward volunteers who had helped out with that and other projects in the city. Gaga and British rock act The Enemy entertained 3,000 volunteers. Gaga spared no detail for the crowd, treating them to exactly the same *Fame Ball* show she'd been touring with.

'When I was a child I dreamed one day of being a star, tonight I want to make everyone who gave up four hours of their time feel like a star – and I can't wait to make them dance their pants off,' she said before the gig. 'I want to make charity and volunteering fashionable and cool. I truly believe in the power of young people, and that music can be a force for good.'

Gaga's Muppet obsession took centre stage when she turned up for an interview on German television wearing a coat made out of *The Muppet Show* character Kermit the Frog. Made by one of Gaga's favourite designers, Jean Charles de Castelbajac, the green furry top was decorated with dozens of Kermits. Gaga even wore a Kermit head fascinator to match the coat.

She had already made headlines with her no-pants policy and addiction to latex. But the Kermit outfit was something from another planet. The media were totally baffled, and it was down to the Lady herself to explain the reason she picked the froggy outfit for her interview. 'I really loved this one … because I thought it was commentary on not wearing fur, because I hate fur and I don't wear fur,' Gaga later told Ryan Seacrest.

In further attempts to explain her fashion choices, Gaga simply told reporters that everything she did was intended to be performance art. 'Everything that you see me do is in some way taken and inspired by these visions in my brain that happen because of the way I live my life,' she said at T in the Park. 'I just live and breathe art every day, and I consider myself to be a performance artist. Every time you see me, it's performance. When I'm sleeping, it's performance.'

Gaga's explanations did not help confused journalists, who were used to sycophantic, shallow celebrities, who were easy paparazzi fodder. These celebs would go out partying, spend ridiculous amounts of money on drugs and alcohol, buy huge cars and beach houses and live conventional celebrity lifestyles. Gaga was a completely alien concept to them. Although she dressed in raunchy outfits, the way she intended to shock was completely different from the average A-lister, who went commando in order to flash the paps while getting out of a car. She made a fashion accessory out of a teacup, and had worn clothing made from the Muppets. Gaga had never thought of herself as conventionally pretty, and she played on that by wearing elaborate outfits and artistic fashion creations that were unlike anything anyone had ever seen.

'I look at photos of myself, and I look like such a tranny! It's amazing!' she joked to *Fab* magazine. 'I look like Grace Jones, androgynous, robo, future fashion queen. It's not what is sexy. It's graphic, and it's art. But that's what's funny: well, yeah, I take my pants off, but does it matter if your pants are off if you've got eight-inch shoulder pads on, and a hood, and black lipstick and glasses with rocks on them? I don't know. That's sexy to me. But I don't really think anybody's d*** is hard looking at that. I think they're just confused, and maybe a little scared.'

Although the mainstream media might have been confused – and a little scared – more and more people noticed how much attention Gaga was getting because of her clothing, and there was another rash of celebrity copycat sightings, one of which was Rihanna, who arrived for Independence Day celebrations with only silver sequinned stars glued to her nipples. She was spotted out again sporting black electrical tape pasties forming an 'X' over each nipple, a look Gaga had sported back in April.

Another Gaga fashion trend – her no-pants rule – was adopted by a number of celebrities, who were spotted out and about in July trying to outdo the chick from New York in big pants and leotards. At T in the Park, a number of female pop stars tried to recreate Gaga's outlandish looks for themselves. Lily Allen performed in leopard-print pants, sparkly tights and a baggy black top, while Katy Perry barely managed to cover her modesty in a tiny tartan outfit.

Daisy Lowe and Zoe Salmon were spotted out on the town wearing leopard-print Agent Provocateur bodysuits, while Pixie Lott and Beyoncé alter ego Sasha Fierce rocked the leotard look onstage. Always one to jump on any style bandwagon, glamour model Jordan wore a gaudy sequin leotard to her book launch, giving us a prime example of how not to wear the look.

The imitations didn't stop there. Romanian pop star twins The Cheeky Girls actually dressed up as Gaga for a photo shoot in *Closer* magazine, wearing blonde wigs, fishnet tights and leotards. 'We're big fans – she's amazing,' Monica gushed to *Closer*. 'We wanted to dress up as Lady Gaga because she's known for her great make-up and clothes. We love dressing up on stage, too – it's part of performing.'

Although many celebrities were using Gaga as their fashion reference, Gaga herself freely admitted to taking inspiration from a number of sources. Experienced music journalists gleefully pointed out that she had effectively borrowed many of her looks from 1970s glamour, artist Andy Warhol and pop stars David Bowie, Grace Jones and the Queen of Pop herself, Madonna. But sources close to one of pop's premier princesses – Britney Spears – said that the 'Toxic' starlet was getting annoyed with Gaga for stealing her looks! Britney had been walking around onstage in her underwear for almost a decade, and was apparently concerned that Gaga was treading on her toes.

'On the one hand, Britney appreciates that Gaga is so into

her look because it shows she respects her, but Britney worries that Gaga is encroaching on her territory,' a source told *Star* magazine. 'As long as it doesn't completely steal her thunder, she's OK with it.'

Fashion blogs commenting on the saga were unconvinced. After all, when was the last time Britney turned up for an interview wearing a coat made entirely out of Kermit the Frog?

Even though the tabloids tried to bait her into retaliating, Gaga refused to bite. She only ever had good things to say about her hero. 'Britney's a real class act in terms of the way she handles herself in the media and embraces new artists,' she said. 'She's always really kind, I've always admired that about her. She's gonna kick everybody's ass. She's awesome. As far as I'm concerned Britney never left.'

Meanwhile, Gaga was having trouble in her personal life again as the distance proved too much of a strain on her relationship with Speedy. Distraught and unable to commit to him with such a hectic schedule, Gaga finished with the model, but wasted no time in finding a replacement in London. The mystery man was snapped having dinner and canoodling with Gaga in Balans restaurant in Soho, though he looked positively pedestrian next to Gaga's intergalactic Alexander McQueen robe, and appeared distinctly uncomfortable sitting next to her in the cab.

As well as canoodling with a mystery man and wishing she was dating Beethoven, Gaga declared herself to be Kanye West's wife: 'I'm married to Kanye, I love and admire him so much. As I say, we're married.'

But Gaga's debauched partying was only an escape from heartbreak and loneliness, and sooner or later it was bound to catch up with her. Splitting from Speedy had brought back all the rawness surrounding her relationship with Lüc, which seemed to belong to another lifetime back in New York.

'Do you know the feeling of your heart being so terribly broken you can feel the blood dripping out? ... when you have felt this, only then can you know how I'm doing,' she spilled to the *Sun*, hinting that she was missing home so much she was going to quit her overseas promotional duties and return to America. 'I'm homesick for New York. I can't tell you how much I miss that city. I love it all: the concrete, the bars, my family and friends.'

Even though she appeared to be running away from a broken heart, Gaga had always maintained that a man was never going to be the answer to her problems. 'I probably won't ever settle down,' she said to Showbiz Spy. 'Part of me would love all that, but the bigger part of me knows it's never going to happen. I don't think I'm cut out for love and marriage. Music and my art are the big things in my life. I know whatever happens they won't cheat on me and they'll never let me down. Men nearly always do.'

Gaga had discovered the hard way that she had to choose between fame and love, because both together would never work. She had broken up with Lüc because he wanted her to stay at home and leave show business, and now she had split up with Speedy because of her hectic touring schedule. Love and work were not compatible in Gaga's world, and never would be.

Chapter Twenty-Three **Late Summer**

Whatever people might have thought about Gaga, one thing was for sure, she didn't let other people's opinions of her love life stop her doing what she wanted to do.

'I don't need a man. I might sometimes want a man, but I don't need one. I earn my money, I create my art, I know where I am going,' she said. 'I think my parents thought I'd be married by now, but I rebelled against that whole life. I'm unconventional, I'm a rebel.'

The *Sun* said Gaga didn't have time for a boyfriend because of her busy schedule, quoting the Lady as saying, 'I am single and a workaholic and very lonely.' In typical Gaga style she then added, 'But I'm good. Me and my vibrator are very happy.'

Not everyone was so sure about that, though. Close friends of the singer were afraid she was heading for a breakdown, thanks to her recent break-up and her inexorable rise to fame.

'Everything seems to have gone wrong at once for her,' a source told *Look* magazine. 'She split up with Speedy last month, and since then I think the toll of relentless touring and promotion over the past year has hit her.

'We're worried she is going to have a breakdown if she keeps going on like this. She's clearly heartbroken and exhausted and she should slow down and look after herself. But even though she says she's ruined her life, it's as if she's addicted to the fame.'

With or without the support of a romantic rock in her life, her records were having a huge impact on the charts. At the end of July she had two songs – 'Poker Face' and 'Just Dance' – in the Top 10 of the Top 50 Digital Songs of All Time list, which was an incredible feat.

The video for 'LoveGame' had racked up more than 18 million views on YouTube and the single had gone to number one in America, making Lady Gaga only the third artist in American history to have three number one songs from a début album. What's more, *The Fame* had been certified Platinum in Australia, the UK and the US.

As a formal recognition of her chart success, Gaga was nominated for no less than nine MTV Video Music Awards – tying her with Beyoncé for most nominations, and giving her two more nominations than Britney Spears. The nominations included Best New Artist; 'Poker Face' for Video of the Year, Best Female Video and Best Pop Video; but it was 'Paparazzi' that got the most attention, with nominations for Best Direction, Best Editing, Best Special Effects, Best Cinematography and Best Art Direction.

'After years of hustle in New York City, where we made our

art videos in bars, myself and the Haus of Gaga are honoured to receive nine nominations for the 2009 VMAs,' she told *MTV News*, before continuing with the bizarre statement: 'We believe in the immensity and the promise of "showbiz" and will continue to give it mouth-to-mouth, till its vomiting return. All you need is a camcorder, a flashlight and one truly great idea. Thank you, MTV, for being our video flagship, and for supporting this bunch of inspired kids, who love to get wasted and make art together.'

The Fame Ball tour was headed for some dates in Asia, and to celebrate her nominations Gaga met up with Perez Hilton in Japan. They headed for a Tokyo beauty parlour, where they enjoyed champagne, manicures and pedicures and a lot of girl talk. And – just to treat herself a little more for her achievement – after a few glasses of champagne, Gaga headed off for a late-night session in a tattoo parlour in Osaka to get some serious ink!

She turned up to her concert in Seoul, South Korea, dressed in a glittering gold dress by Korean designer Lie Sang Bong, with the tattoo fully healed and on display for all to see on her left bicep. The tattoo was a quote from her favourite philosopher, Rainer Maria Rilke, and it read, 'In the deepest hour of the night, confess to yourself that you would die if you were forbidden to write. And look deep into your heart where it spreads its roots, the answer, and ask yourself, must I write?'

Gaga had always felt like she connected with Rilke's philosophy of solitude, which she felt was present in her life as a musician. 'Solitude is something you marry, as an artist,' she wrote on Twitter. 'When you are an artist, your solitude is a lonely place that you embrace.'

Although Gaga spent much of her time onstage prancing

around wearing next to nothing, her style agenda was very different for the next leg of her tour, playing a show in Tel Aviv and visiting Jerusalem.

Having attended a religious school in her youth, Gaga believed in God and considered herself religious, so she was really excited about seeing the sacred holy city of Jerusalem. Out of respect, she covered herself up in a modest outfit of black trousers, a black top, headscarf and crucifix as she visited the Western Wall in the Old City, although in typical Gaga fashion, while performing onstage, she told everyone in the audience that she wanted them to go home and make love to each other.

Her outlandish behaviour continued as she returned to the UK to play V Festival. And she was spotted on the plane back to the UK from Tel Aviv getting close to a mystery man – none other than her creative director, Matty Dada Williams. But a source close to Gaga denied that the couple were anything more than friends, saying that that was just how the pop princess acted with people she was close to.

When the plane landed at Heathrow, Gaga kept the paparazzi waiting as she stayed on the plane, adjusting her outfit, much to the dismay of the flight attendants, who had to wait for her to finish. Half an hour later she emerged with fake fangs and long fake nails, designed to shock, of course. Needless to say it worked and she was in the gossip pages of almost every major website within an hour of her arrival.

The *Twilight*-inspired look no doubt came from a photo shoot she had just done with Ellen von Unwerth for the cover of gay magazine *Out*. Gaga got to explore her love of B-movies and monsters, as Ellen dressed her as a vampire and a zombie for the photo shoot.

The day after flying into Britain, she was spotted at London's exclusive Percy & Reed salon, where she spent a leisurely five hours having her hair, nails, fake tan and extensions done for her performance at V Festival. Ever the demanding diva, she requested that an entire floor of the salon be sealed off for her pampering session, and even wore her sunglasses to the toilet while she was there. In preparation for the festival, she had not one but three sprays in a St Tropez self-tanning booth, aiming for that truly neon glow she had become famous for.

To add to the pre-show madness, as part of her backstage rider requests for V Festival she demanded organisers have a purple cup full of English tea ready for her at all times! The Virgin Media Louder Lounge announced their plans to lay on sparkly brownies to go with the tea.

Perhaps it was the brownies that distracted her, because twenty minutes after she was meant to take the stage, she still hadn't appeared. The crowd started stamping their feet and booing, but as they started a slow handclap, the lights dimmed and the Lady appeared onstage. The crowd went wild, screaming and shouting for her, but the performance ended badly. Because she'd gone onstage late, the organisers wouldn't let her finish her set; she only managed to play the acoustic version of 'Poker Face' on her piano before they pulled the plug on her – to a chorus of boos and jeers.

Distraught, Gaga took to Twitter twice to apologise to her fans. 'My fans were lovely and really deserved to hear poker-face. I love you and I'm sorry,' she said initially, following the sentiment with, 'Stage manager pulled the plug because I was 5 minutes over my time at V fest. Show was incredible. A shame people have no respect for music.'

That wasn't the last scandal Gaga would face over the

summer. In fact, it seemed like people were lining up to take a pop at her. Irish singer Roisin Murphy was reported by the *Daily Express* as telling the British media that the New York singer had stolen her look, allegedly saying, 'She's copied my style. I met her about a year ago before she got really big and I had no clue that this was all going to happen. She wasn't wearing shoulder pads at the time and I was. Lady Gaga is just a poor imitation of me. She has copied my style, she took my shoulder pads and all that. Mind you, she doesn't wear the bottom half!'

In characteristic Gaga style, she didn't respond to the comments, which were refuted by Murphy the very next day!

'I NEVER said, "Lady Gaga is a poor imitation of me." That was a completely made-up quote!' Murphy said in a statement. 'I respect Lady Gaga's work as an artist and as a fellow fashion icon. She is a very talented performer, playing the piano, singing live and dancing too … All the best to Lady Gaga – she is fantastic.'

With one controversy cleared up, another scandal followed hot on its heels – this time involving singer-songwriter Tori Amos, who weighed into the Gaga debate. Amos started a celebrity feud between herself and the singer in the *Sun*, who quoted her as saying, 'She's what I call a meteor – singers who entertain people for a while. Hey, there's nothing wrong with that … The question is, will Lady Gaga be playing alongside Neil Young at Glastonbury in twenty years time? She wants to entertain people. Right now, half the world is depressed and they need to be entertained. So her timing's perfect.'

Whether those words were accurate or not, Amos didn't take the *Sun* to task over the quote. But again Gaga refused to comment. She knew that the press – the British tabloids particularly - were fond of making up rumours and stories just to sell papers. Besides which, she never compared her success to anyone else's, and refused to be drawn into a media battle with anyone.

There was one issue, however, that called for her to speak out - a scandal that had been bubbling away quietly for some time. It involved allegations that she wasn't a woman but, in fact, a hermaphrodite, with both male and female sexual organs.

Chapter Twenty-Four
Hermaphrodite Rumours

Rumours about Gaga's sexuality and gender had been flying around cyberspace for just under a year, since 11 November 2008, when Christina Aguilera had commented that she didn't know whether Gaga was a man or a woman.

As a big supporter of the gay and alternative community, Gaga embraced fans calling her style 'trannylicious', and said that she had been heavily influenced by the drag scene. This background, coupled with a sighting of Gaga's alleged penis, led to widespread rumours that she was, in fact, a she-he.

The story burned through the Internet like wildfire, starting when someone posted a video of her performance at Glastonbury, when she was telling the crowd a story before the start of 'Money Honey'. She was lying on one of her scooters while her dancers wheeled her over to the far side of the stage, and when she came to get off, she swung her leg over while facing forwards and said under her breath, 'I don't think I have panties on.'

Someone misheard what she said and mistook it for a penis reference. Screenshots of the video were posted on forums, with fans circling Gaga's alleged penis, though clearly, on closer inspection, it was nothing more than camel toe.

Further fuelling the fire, a quote then appeared on a number of fan websites, allegedly attributed to Lady Gaga herself, although it was impossible to trace the original source of the quote: *'It's not something that I'm ashamed of, just isn't something that i go around telling everyone,' read the comment. 'Yes. I have both male and female genitalia, but i consider myself a female. Its just a little bit of a penis and really doesnt interfere much with my life. the reason I haven't talked about it is that its not a big deal to me. like come on. its not like we all go around talking about our vags. I think this is a great opportunity to make other multiple gendered people feel more comfortable with their bodies. I'm sexy, I'm hot. i have both a poon and a peener. big fucking deal.'*

At first, Gaga found the whole thing funny and took it as a joke. She had spoken openly of her bisexuality in the past, and when Jonathan Ross had brought up Christina Aguilera's comments about not knowing whether Gaga was a man or a woman, she had joked, 'I have a really big donkey dick.'

During an acoustic rendition of 'Poker Face' at the concert in Manila, she spoke out about it to the audience: 'Somebody asked me very recently a very strange question. They said, "Lady Gaga, do you have a d**k?" and I said, "Yes I do, it's much bigger than yours."' The crowd went wild and screamed and shouted for her.

The controversy attracted endless amounts of attention, some unwanted. ABC News even managed to call Troy Carter, Gaga's manager, to get a comment on the issue, but Troy wasn't playing, and considered it an absurd ploy by the newspapers. Troy called the quote and the rumours completely ridiculous, but even that wasn't enough to kill the story.

The *Daily Mirror* reported that even Katy Perry had poo-pooed the rumours about her friend. 'Oh, please. It's all very calculated,' Katy apparently told the paper. 'She knows what she's doing. She put something in her knickers, a mini strap-on. Bless her if she does have a d***, but I am certain she doesn't.'

In actual fact, there was no way Katy could have made that comment as she was on a twenty-four-hour flight from Australia when the newspaper printed the story. Perez Hilton leapt to Katy's defence, stating on Twitter that Katy had never given any interviews to the British media talking about Lady Gaga being a hermaphrodite, and that the British press were out of control.

Finally the rumour was starting to get on Gaga's nerves. The MTV Video Music Awards were creeping up, but rather than being excited and doing a lot of press for that, she was having to go over and over this ridiculous story constantly. So when she was asked about the rumour again in a phone interview with the Australian radio programme, *The Matt & Jo Show*, in early September, she shot it down then and there. 'It's too low brow for me to even discuss,' she said. 'I've made fun of it before but to talk about it is ridiculous. I'm an accomplished musician and I'd much rather talk about my fans and my music.'

At a press conference in Germany for the launch of her new Heartbeats headphones, Gaga was angered by German TV personality Collien Fernandes, who continued to push the issue, asking if Gaga had a penis. 'My vagina is offended by this question,' Gaga said angrily before Collien was thrown out of the press conference by security.

'I don't really understand the fuss,' Collien said afterwards. 'It's obvious someone would ask her this question after the picture was all over the news.'

'My beautiful vagina is very offended. I'm not offended – my vagina is offended,' Gaga retorted. 'I've sold four million records in six months. I'm not embarrassed about anything.'

In fact, the chick from New York had her own explanations about everyone's obsession with her genitalia: 'I think more than anything, it's society's reaction to a strong woman,' she said to *MTV News*. 'The idea that we equate strength with men and a penis is a symbol of male strength, you know, it's just what it is. But like I said, I'm not offended at all, but my vagina might be a little bit upset.'

If the rumours about her sexuality weren't confusing enough, there was another bizarre headline that her fans had to digest – that she had been enlisted by crooner Michael Bolton to write some material for his new album.

'I was taking a break from production when my manager and the label tag-teamed me on the phone about writing with a young artist named Lady Gaga who I had never heard of but they were raving about. They said that she was a huge fan of mine and wanted to write with me,' Bolton told *Metro*.

Listening to some of her records, he was instantly won over, and knew she was going to be a huge hit. As for Gaga, she was just happy to be able to get into a different style of songwriting.

'I love Michael Bolton, and I always have,' she gushed to *Newsweek*. 'I looked at it as an exciting opportunity … It was always dance music. It was an exciting opportunity to work with someone as timeless as Michael and do a ballad. Do something that I'm really good at that I don't get to show very much.'

With the tabloids reeling from the hermaphrodite rumours and Gaga's strange partnership with Michael Bolton, the Haus of Gaga were quietly preparing themselves for the performance of a lifetime. She was scheduled to perform at the MTV Video Music Awards, and every member of the Haus had been hard at work designing a stage set-up, a dance routine and a performance that would go down in VMA history.

'I sort of have this philosophy about things: there's never a reason to do something unless it's going to be memorable, unless it's going to change things, unless it's going to inspire a movement,' Gaga said to *Newsweek*. 'With the song and with the performance, I hope to say something very grave about fame and the price of it.' She was very tight-lipped about what she was actually going to do onstage, only disclosing that she would perform a recent single, but with a different and more dramatic interpretation, rooted in New York-style performance art.

'It's less of me singing the song, and more of an art installation,' she continued. 'It's very well designed and thought out, and we've been planning it for months and months. It is for me a very meaningful performance, [for] where I am in my career, as well as the experiences I've had.'

Regardless of whether she managed to bag any VMAs or not, there was great news for Gaga on the chart front. On 6 September, she was officially crowned queen of downloads, as 'Poker Face' became the most downloaded song since the download chart had started five years earlier. According to the Official UK Charts Company, 'Poker Face' racked up 779,000 sales on downloads alone to top the chart, while her début single 'Just Dance' came in at the third most downloaded, with 700,000 sales.

'I am honoured to be the songwriter and performer behind the number one and number three all-time most downloaded songs in history in the UK,' Gaga said, over the moon at how incredibly well her tracks were doing in Britain. She had a great respect for many innovative British artists and a big soft spot for her British fans.

Obsessed by making music, Gaga was still finding time to write music while on the road. 'I just wrote a song for my re-release, which is called "The Fame Monster",' she confirmed on MTV Playground. 'I believe that in fashion and in music and in art everything is going in this dark direction, and so I wrote a song called "Monster". The idea that life after *The Fame* happens is a monstrous life, a life of horror. So building on that idea of 1950s monster movies – for some people they think it's a bit wacky, but for the Haus, we think it's beautiful.'

With plans put in place for *The Fame Kills* co-headlining tour with Kanye West, and the wheels in motion for *The Fame Monster* album re-release in November, Gaga could put all her focus on preparing for the MTV VMAs.

Her rehearsals were well-guarded, with only one representative from MTV – VMA creative director Lee Lodge – being allowed in to watch. Everyone was expecting something amazing from Gaga; they just didn't know what.

The big night – 13 September – was finally here, and as well as a killer performance, Gaga had some amazing outfits ready for the show. She might not win any awards, but she would make damn sure that people would remember her presence.

Gaga arrived in style for one of the most unexpected

red-carpet entrances of the night, with none other than Muppet Kermit the Frog as her date. In an attempt not to be upstaged, Gaga wore a gold neck brace and gold face mask with black feathers by Jean Paul Gaultier. Although Kermit didn't get out of the limo, Gaga made sure to kiss her date goodbye, leaning in through the window and giving him a kiss.

'He's been a really good date,' she told *MTV News* on the red carpet. 'It's our first date, but we've been eyeing each other for a while.'

Although she wasn't on the red carpet, Madonna caught Gaga's first outfit, and thought she looked fresh. 'I just saw Lady Gaga,' she said with a smile. 'She looks like she's going to carnival in Venice, very beautiful.'

When *MTV News* asked if she felt threatened by the comparisons, Madonna said: 'No, I'm very flattered.'

Madonna was the star of the opening of the show, with her heartfelt speech paying tribute to Michael Jackson, followed by a group of dancers who performed to a medley of Michael's songs.

Gaga made everyone giddy with her costume changes as everyone tried to keep track of what she was wearing, from the black feathered outfit to a white lace dress and huge lace headpiece that looked like mouse ears, to a translucent white panel dress with a bizarre feather snood that made her look a little like a lion, to a pearly leotard and then a red lace bodystocking.

The costume changes didn't detract from her achievements, though. Gaga snagged herself three 'Moonmen' (the slang for an MTV award): for Best New Artist ('Poker Face'), Best Special Effects ('Paparazzi') and Best Art Direction ('Paparazzi').

Gaga and the Haus were over the moon about their awards,

and all around the country members of Team Gaga screamed and shouted. The Lady had come good.

Looking back on her second single, it's amazing that 'Poker Face' was so successful, given how troublesome the two dogs were during filming of the video. But director Ray Kay knew that the magic was down to one thing only: the special artist that Gaga was.

'That video is so much Gaga,' he said. 'She was the one who made the video so unique. I was just trying to help her create that world. So many people think artists are just products of the record industry or there are people behind them that create looks for them. But she's the best example of anyone I've ever seen of someone who really created their own style and really *is* that personae. She is amazing,' he gushed to *MTV News*.

The video shoot for 'Paparazzi' hadn't been perfect either, and yet here they were, with two VMA awards for it. 'It was a bit stressful,' Gaga remembered. 'I was screaming at everyone all day because it was so detailed and so intricate and I really wanted it to be documented properly, especially when these designers like Mugler send you these amazing archives, they have to be shot well. But Jonas Åckerlund is one of the best directors on the planet, and me and the Haus worked on the treatment for months and months.'

'It's really inspired by certain social themes – social death, fame whoring, pornography and murder. I think pornography and murder are some of the most desperate cries for attention and fame in the world. When murderers or serial killers kill, they leave a trail, or they give themselves a name, or they go back to the crime scene. For me, this is what the video needed to be about. It needed to add a layer of what the media can really do to the artist. Social death and what it implies. So that's what the video is about.' And these were all the themes that she had taken and spun around for her live show.

It wasn't the awards that the show would be remembered for, though. Taking the stage for her performance, Gaga gave what would go down in MTV history as one of the most impressive stage shows ever.

Flanked by male and female dancers all dressed in white, and Gaga herself in knee-high white boots, fishnets, a white bra top and a white beaded mask with huge feather horns, Gaga sang a few lines from 'Poker Face' before bursting into an energetic version of 'Paparazzi', her favourite track from *The Fame* and the video that had won her two prestigious awards.

At points in the song she staggered around the stage with a cane, while a dancer wheeled herself around in a wheelchair like the one in the video. Gaga then danced to the piano, where she thrashed at the keyboard, banging down on the keys with her hands and a foot. She then stood up and staggered across the stage, still singing, when suddenly blood began to pour through her white bra top and drip down her torso. She clutched at the blood, smearing it over her hands, face and hair, then dropped to the floor in a heap. Her dancers lifted her up, then she was hoisted above them by a rope, where she hung, staring at the audience, covered in blood while a golden halo was projected on the big screen behind her.

The audience went completely crazy, screaming and shouting. No one was in their seats when they applauded – the whole building exploded with cheers and clapping.

It was an art masterpiece; exactly what she'd wanted it to be. She dedicated the dramatic performance of 'Paparazzi' to her fans: 'I wanted to say something honest and real and not just give a performance where I was jacking off onstage the whole time about my record. It was really for my fans, who I knew would be at home cheering and swooning,' she said.

Although she undoubtedly gave the performance of the night, other big winners included Beyoncé and Green Day, who each won three awards, and Britney. But the good vibrations were destroyed when Kanye West stormed the stage, and interrupted Taylor Swift's acceptance speech. He snatched the microphone from her hand and started to rant about how much better Beyoncé's video was than Taylor's. Kanye and girlfriend Amber Rose had been drinking heavily before the show began, and it was clear that he was out of his head when he took to the stage.

After security had escorted him off stage, he stuck his fingers up at the crowd, who were booing him. Even celebrities had to be restrained – Pink walked by Kanye, shaking her head in disgust, and had to be escorted away by security before she started a fight with him. Kanye and Amber left the ceremony early, and weren't seen at any after parties.

Many people dismissed Kanye's actions as a publicity stunt. He had a history of losing his cool at the VMAs. Back in 2006 at the MTV Europe Music Awards, his video 'Touch The Sky' lost out to Justice Vs Simian's 'We Are Your Friends'.

'And then at the VMAs in Las Vegas he indulged in a backstage rant after losing in all five of the categories he'd been nominated in,' wrote the *NME*. '"I lost to the f***ing Black Eyed Peas last year, man. I'm never f***ing coming back to MTV." Except he did. Obviously. Because he knows he makes headlines every time he does.'

Everyone initially thought Kanye's actions were a joke, but they soon worked out that he was for real. 'He was very drunk when he did it, but that still doesn't excuse his behaviour,'

Perez Hilton said to *MTV News*. 'I remember reading in interviews him saying he didn't used to drink, and now he's drinking a lot and when someone does things like that it's usually out of desperation … but Kanye doesn't have to be desperate. He's incredibly talented and successful.' Besides which, as Perez also pointed out, it was great publicity, both for Kanye, and for the VMAs. 'At the end of the day people love this,' he added. 'Everyone's talking about it, and that's what they want.'

After the after parties had finished and the media had picked over the pieces of the show, Kanye took to Twitter many times to apologise for his actions, as well as appearing on Jay Leno and other American programmes to say sorry for his behaviour. He took some time out to relax and recuperate because, after all, it was time to start preparing for his co-headlining tour with Gaga: The Fame Kills tour. He might have hit an all-time low with his assault on Taylor Swift's speech, but he was going to win all his fans back – and get some new ones in the process – with the spectacle that would greet them later that year.

Chapter Twenty-Five
The Fame Monster

Though Gaga and the Haus had already started rehearsing for Fame Kills in their large warehouse space in LA, to some observers it seemed like the tour was doomed by Kanye's drunken outburst at the VMAs.

Since the awards, the mystery surrounding the tour was growing. Fame Kills had promised to deliver a visual extravaganza that threatened to revolutionise the spectacle of pop. With the combined talents of Gaga's 'pop-art' pop sensitivities and Kanye's electric urban showmanship, Fame Kills was likely to have been the musical event to eclipse all others in 2009/10.

In the aftermath of the VMAs, Kanye appeared on a number of TV shows to apologise publicly for his outburst, leading many to doubt whether he would be able to pull himself together in time for the first date. The rumour mill was finally put to rest, when, at the start of October, Gaga and Kanye announced that they had taken the mutual decision to cancel Fame Kills for the foreseeable future.

Worried that he was losing his grip on reality, Kanye had decided to turn his back on fame and the high life for a few weeks and chill out – perhaps he was worried he might suffer the same fate as the tour's name suggests.

The cancellation of the tour wasn't the only controversy stirred up by the VMAs. Back in New York, sources reported that the nuns at Sacred Heart, the Catholic school that Gaga had attended, were 'shocked and displeased' by her mock-suicide performance onstage.

Gaga's performance also piqued the interest of more of the world's stars, who were slowly joining Team Gaga. *The X Factor* judge Cheryl Cole told *Grazia* magazine, 'I'm such a big fan of Lady Gaga's style because she's so brave and the real deal – I'm fascinated by how she dresses.' Cheryl was so taken with the style that she channelled Gaga on her '3 Words' video, by wearing a long blonde wig and black veil.

Cheryl wasn't the only celebrity showing appreciation for the New York popstress. Ashley Tisdale, Taylor Swift and even Lindsay Lohan were among the A-listers tweeting about how much they loved Gaga's tunes.

As well as getting a lot of love from celebrities, Gaga was gaining official recognition. She won Best Video at the Q Awards for 'Just Dance', and was honoured for her intuitive and off-the-wall fashion sense with a Stylemaker award from the Accessories Council. Not only was she recognised for her contributions to music and fashion, she was also recognised for her incredible achievements as a woman at *Billboard* magazine's annual Women in Music event. Held in Gaga's hometown of New York, the awards named Gaga as Up and Coming Artist of the Year, while Beyoncé received the Woman of the Year award.

Sources who saw the two pop divas – who were sitting just tables away from each other – reported that they chatted away together after the awards had been presented. Beyoncé had long admired Gaga's individual sense of style and showmanship, and while they were talking, she suggested it would be great if the pair were to collaborate on a project, perhaps contributing vocals for tracks on each other's album. Glancing over their shoulders to ensure they weren't overheard, they agreed to meet up a few days later in a New York studio to work on a new track Beyoncé had started.

The Fame Kills tour might have been cancelled, but Gaga was keeping herself busy. She was disappointed not to be able to execute her plans with Kanye, but she had been considering doing a solo tour in March 2010 anyway, so just decided to bring the dates forward and set off round the world on her own.

'Still leaving on solo TOUR this nov,' she typed out on her BlackBerry and posted to Twitter, but her good mood was tempered when she got an email through from her label telling her that the new single – 'Bad Romance' – had been leaked online. It was an early, and quite rough, demo version, but Gaga was fuming nonetheless. She got straight back on Twitter, telling her fans the leaked version was making her ears bleed.

She had been planning to début the single on the comedy TV show *Saturday Night Live*, on which she was guest-starring. But if viewers weren't completely surprised by the music, most were gobsmacked to see Gaga joined in a comedy skit by the Queen of Pop, Madonna herself. The pair mock-squabbled with each other in one of the show's comedy skits, in which Madonna asked Gaga, 'What the hell is a disco stick?' Making the audience hoot with laughter. Gaga totally upstaged the show's presenter, Ryan Reynolds, and her performance was another victory notch on her bedpost.

Madonna wasn't the only star that Gaga cosied up to in October 2009. After her initial chat to Beyoncé about the pair collaborating on material, Gaga headed to a top-secret studio in New York to work on the video for the track 'Video Phone'. As well as showcasing some incredible fashion creations, 'Video Phone' saw Gaga channelling the ex-Destiny's Child star, with long, flowing locks and wearing a white leotard for the choreographed dance scenes.

'When I was doing her video with her, she called me and she said, "What do you want to do?",' Gaga explained. 'And I'm like, "I don't want to show up in some frickin' hair bow and be fashion Gaga in your video. I want to do you. I want to do my version of Beyoncé." So the whole time I was learning the choreography, they were calling me Gee-yoncé!'

Gaga's touch – turning everything into gold – was even making her friends in the Haus of Gaga sparkle by association. Her DJ, glamorous party girl Lady Starlight, jetted into London to headline a Halloween party that was being held at a secret location. Her 'shopping list' of a rider made Mariah Carey's demands look modest. Starlight's tongue-in-cheek list reportedly contained, amongst other things: a mixed sushi platter served on ice; one bottle of Krug Rose champagne, chilled; five bottles of Jack Daniel's; a fresh fruit platter of yellow and orange fruits only, including star fruit and passion fruit; a pole and two female dancers (one blonde, one brunette, both at least 5'8"); full-length mirrors on every wall of the room, including the ceiling; three bottles of alkyl nitrites; assorted sex toys; two baby hedgehogs and a persian cat; a star registered under Lady Starlight's name; limited-edition Iron Maiden *Sound House Tapes* 7" vinyl; a fan in every room and a smoke machine. Never one to miss the chance for a party, Starlight rocked the roof off the Halloween show.

Unfortunately though, Gaga, who was back in America, couldn't make the party. Even though she had been a smash at the VMAs and received a number of awards, things at home had taken a darker turn. First of all, she was deeply upset by the news that Rumpus – one of the Harlequin Great Danes that had featured in her videos – had passed away aged only five years old. Gaga had planned to use Rumpus and his mother in more video and film projects, and the whole Haus mourned the dog's death.

Rumpus wasn't the only strange death to haunt the Haus as 2009 drew to a close. When Gaga attended the ACE Awards, she wore a widow-like black veil over her face. She stepped onto the red carpet and sashayed towards the entrance to the building, and just a minute later, celebrity photographer A.J. Sokalner collapsed right in front of her. He had been working the red carpet that night taking pictures of all the celebs. After suffering a heart attack, he collapsed and was then rushed to hospital, where he was pronounced dead shortly after.

Although Gaga hadn't known the photographer personally, many newspapers and websites pointed to her widow's veil, wondering if her outfit and the death were somehow related. Of course the Haus knew this wasn't true, but they couldn't help but feel that something eerie was afoot. Gaga had been told as a youngster that bad things always happened in threes, and she was scared of what the third thing might be.

Just a few days later she found out, and it was far worse than she could have imagined. Her father had been complaining of chest pains and was rushed to hospital, where it transpired he would need to undergo a serious operation. Gaga instantly demanded that she pay for it. 'I haven't bought anything yet with any of the money that I've made from my new album,' she begged her father, 'so let me buy you a new heart, Dad.'

Her father turned to look at his eldest daughter's determined face. 'OK, fine,' he answered her.

'It was pretty necessary,' she explained later. 'It was the biggest nightmare of my life. My father is my whole world; I'm such a daddy's girl.'

She updated her fans on the situation via Twitter while spending time with her dad at the hospital. 'My Daddy had open heart surgery today. And after long hours, and lots of tears, they healed his broken heart, and mine. Speechless,' she typed on her BlackBerry. She updated later with, 'At the hospital. Giving daddy a footrub while he falls asleep. He's my hero.'

Safe in the knowledge that her father was in good hands and recovering well, Gaga was able to turn her attention to promoting *The Fame Monster*. Initially, she had planned to re-release her début album *The Fame* as a deluxe package containing eight new songs, including lead single 'Bad Romance'.

All the new material had been written while she was on the road, travelling around the world for the past two years. She had made the decision to write about everything she didn't write about on *The Fame*. 'I never really decided what I wanted to write about at all,' she said. 'I just felt this urgency to write about what I was going through – my fears and my monsters.

I had been so ambitious and dreaming for so long that I wasn't feeling very much.'

These monsters had mostly come to Gaga as she travelled through Europe promoting *The Fame*. She had taken a number of different influences and combined them into an electronic pulse for her new material. *The Fame Monster* was born as a pop experiment, with components of industrial, Goth beats, 1990s dance melodies and her obsession with the lyrical genius of 1980s melancholic pop and the runway. 'I wrote while watching muted fashion shows and I am compelled to say my music was scored for them,' she explained.

Working on the look of *The Fame Monster* was almost as important to Gaga as working on the music itself. She wanted to make sure that it retained a darker, more edgy feel than *The Fame*, because although it was comprised of the same intelligent electro-pop, it had come from a different place creatively.

'I had lots of arguments with my record labels about my album covers because they were sort of classic and simple,' Gaga said to *MTV News*. 'And there's this one image of me with very dark hair, crying, and they're like, "It's so dark and no-body's going to understand".' But Gaga knew not to underestimate her fans. She knew they would understand it, and understand her. She had every faith in them.

To put the new album together, Gaga had collaborated with her old buddy RedOne who, after becoming a daddy, was just getting back to work. Having produced most of *The Fame*, RedOne had a great working relationship with Gaga, which was bound to produce some serious beats. As well as RedOne, Gaga called on some other producers she knew and trusted to work on the rest of the material with her, including pop and urban industry heavyweights like Teddy Riley, Rodney Jerkins, Ron Fair and Fernando Garibay.

Although mainly synthesiser driven, the eight tracks varied in style. RedOne worked with Gaga on the stomping lead single 'Bad Romance', which was recorded and produced in Amsterdam, and which features a cutting-edge, futuristic video. RedOne also worked on epic pop ballad 'Alejandro' and club smash 'Monster' (which was written about Gaga's fear of attachment, and fear of loving something that's bad for you: 'If you listen to the lyrics, it's like being in love with the bad boy all the time, and you keep going back for more,' she explained). RedOne also helped write the more relaxed pop tune 'So Happy I Could Die', a song about being happy in a club drinking none other than Gaga's favourite tipple, red wine (of course).

Gaga's favourite song on the album is the ballad 'Speechless', which she wrote about the possibility of losing her father. 'My mom called me and I was very depressed,' Gaga said. 'I was on tour and I couldn't leave, so I went into the studio and I wrote this song "Speechless," and it's about these phone calls. My dad used to call me after he'd had a few drinks and I wouldn't know what to say. I was speechless and I just feared that I would lose him and I wouldn't be there.'

Laced with club tracks, *The Fame Monster* was definitely designed to get people dancing. 'Telephone' was initially earmarked as a single for Britney, but luckily for Gaga fans, the New York chick made 'Telephone' entirely her own – with a little help from new buddy Beyoncé. The diva combination had worked well on Beyoncé's 'Video Phone', and came across even more strongly in 'Telephone'. The fans seemed to agree, too, as the addictive tune hit the top of the playback charts in countries across the world.

Forever mindful of being generous to her fans, Gaga decided to release *The Fame Monster* in a number of different formats. In Europe it was released as an additional disc to her début, *The Fame*, while in the US *The Fame Monster* was available as a stand-alone CD. For the fans who had more cash to flash, Gaga provided an even more exciting album experience with a limited-edition digipak version. While for her super-rich, super-dedicated fans she released a deluxe collector's edition art book. Offering the ultimate peek inside the Haus of Gaga, it spanned music, fashion, art and gossip, and included the eight new tracks, pictures, posters, puzzles, the original album *The Fame*, fanzines, an individually numbered *Book of Gaga*, a paper doll collection, a note from Gaga herself and even a lock of her hair!

The decision to release the art book was pure Gaga. Needless to say the fans loved it, and the book sold out within days of being available as a pre-order. Her fans just couldn't get enough of her music, as evidenced when 'Bad Romance' went straight to number nine on the *Billboard* Hot 100 in America, making it her fifth Top 10 single in America, while 'Paparazzi' remained at number six.

While 'Bad Romance' was doing well in the digital download chart, the video had already received thousands of views. It had been shot to capture the essence of a tough female spirit, as Gaga finds herself kidnapped by a group of jealous supermodels.

'There's this one shot in the video where I get kidnapped by supermodels,' she explained. 'I'm washing away my sins and they shove vodka down my throat to drug me up before they sell me off to the Russian mafia.'

The most controversial aspect of the video, however, was

the razor-blade sunglasses. Gaga explained a little more about them: 'I wanted to design a pair for some of the toughest chicks, and some of my girlfriends – don't do this at home! – they used to keep razor blades in the side of their mouths. That tough female spirit is something that I want to project. It's meant to be, "This is my shield, this is my weapon, this is my inner sense of fame, this is my monster."'

The Fame Monster sold hundreds of thousands of copies, as eager fans around the world grabbed whatever format they could while they eagerly waited for *The Fame Monster* tour to get underway.

As a warm-up before the tour started, Gaga flew to LA to perform at the Los Angeles Museum of Contemporary Art at its annual fundraiser. There she joined celebs like Brad Pitt, Angelina Jolie, Eva Mendes, Gwen Stefani and Jessica Alba wandering through the galleries filled with works by Jackson Pollock and Gaga's hero, Andy Warhol.

Gaga's performance art piece, however, entitled 'The Shortest Musical You Will Never See Again', upstaged all the artwork on display. It was orchestrated by artist Francesco Vezzoli and featured Lady Gaga in the starring role, playing piano and singing *The Fame Monster* song 'Speechless' on a rotating pink Steinway piano painted by Damien Hirst. Members of Russia's Bolshoi Ballet danced alongside, while Vezzoli performed an interpretive needlepoint as Gaga sang. It was quite a spectacle, and the entire audience was mesmerised by it.

It was a million miles away from the tour she was about to embark on, but she had the chance to put in some early practice at the American Music Awards. Performing 'Bad Romance' and 'Speechless', Gaga donned a nude bodysuit and climbed into a perspex box to play the piano. Her piano then burst into flames, and she was surrounded by violin players wearing gas masks. Although Gaga didn't win any awards, she was the name on everyone's lips after the show.

But as Gaga flew to Montreal for the first date of her headline tour, she was still fending off rumours that she had fallen out with Kanye about the Fame Kills tour. Many people were wondering whether she would be taking aspects of their collaboration on the road with her for The Fame Monster tour, but Gaga was adamant that she was respectful of her partnership with Kanye. 'I'm certainly inspired by what we were doing, but I made a decision based on integrity not to use any of the things that we had designed together,' she said to *Rolling Stone* magazine.

'It just wasn't the right timing [to go on tour with West]. I don't want to embellish on it too much because I want to respect Kanye's privacy, but we just had our own reasons. We're real friends, real friends can make decisions like that, and we wanted to keep the momentum going in terms of pop music staying innovative with hip-hop and R&B, and we really wanted to do it, and it just wasn't the right time. But who's to say what will happen in the future?'

Gaga and the Haus had put a lot of time and effort into designing a new show that would put all their past efforts to shame. 'I've designed a stage with Haus of Gaga that is essentially a frame with forced perspective, and the frame is put inside the stage,' she said cryptically. About the tour's conception, she explained that the Haus 'started talking about evolution and the evolution of humanity and how we begin as one thing, and we become another'.

There was a great air of secrecy surrounding the tour. The

Haus of Gaga had refused to allow any press to come and see previews of the show, nor had they allocated press tickets for the shows. They didn't need to. Following the Kanye West fallout, the tour had become hugely oversubscribed, with arenas selling out in hours. And Gaga made sure that her show lived up to all the hype.

After the support acts had left the stage, Gaga hid from the crowd behind a video screen. Lit up by green lasers, and dressed in a space-age silver bejewelled jumpsuit (and co-ordinating makeup, of course), she kicked off the show with new song 'Dance In The Dark' from *The Fame Monster*. She was a shock of energy on the stage, strapping on her silver keyboard and strutting across the stage, and disappearing between songs for costume changes that included nude bodysuits, gold gowns, gold Cleopatra-style head-dresses, strappy black leather garments and a black feathered jacket. Gaga did skip offstage for a lot of costume changes, but with dancers on stage, videos projected onto huge screens and a full band to entertain, no one seemed to mind her constantly rotating wardrobe.

And although the dance tracks like 'Just Dance' and 'Poker Face' got everybody moving, there was a good change of pace throughout the show, as Gaga took to the piano for ballads like 'Speechless', and also for the acoustic version of 'Poker Face'.

But it wasn't the outfits or the tunes that first hit the headlines about the tour. Once again, it was Gaga's risqué performances onstage that got some fingers wagging and tongues tutting. Never one to shy away from her sexuality, Gaga spread her legs while straddling a chair during 'Paper Gangsta', and the perceived ménage à trois that occurred onstage caused an outrage in the newspapers that covered the event. During 'Alejandro', Gaga was even carried across the stage by one of her male dancers who was just holding her up by her crotch. In another stage routine, her breasts were groped – by her, and again by one of her male dancers!

But of course, Gaga knew what she was doing. She had combined the sensuality and energy of youth today, and her audience screamed and screamed for more when she performed the show's closing track, 'Bad Romance', dressed in a white marching-band style power jacket and high-waisted pants.

The tour was a great success, not only for Gaga herself, but it was a triumph for all of those who worked tirelessly behind the scenes on the show. It raised the profile of the Haus of Gaga, which remains one of the most mysterious design teams working in the music industry today. As well as designing and making all her costumes, the secret group form Gaga's backbone – her pop-life family, if you like. 'They're my best friends,' she said. 'I'm not really sure what the world thinks ... but I do hear things like, "Who is the Haus of Gaga?" and, "Are you putting out a fashion line?" And no one gets it. It's not a commodity. It's not something that's meant to be sold.'

'It's a real bond and relationship, and that's what I think music and art is about,' she went on. 'They are my heart and soul. They believe in me, and they look at me like a mother and daughter and sister, with pride and love.'

Gaga knew the tour would offer her fans an experience they would never forget, but as she finished her first few shows and took the tour into 2010, the question on everyone's lips was simple: how could she ever top this?